HENRY JAMES'S CRITICISM

HENRY JAMES'S CRITICISM

BY

MORRIS ROBERTS

1970

OCTAGON BOOKS

New York

Reprinted 1970
by special arrangement with Harvard University Press

OCTAGON BOOKS
A DIVISION OF FARRAR, STRAUS & GIROUX, INC.
19 Union Square West
New York, N. Y. 10003

LIBRARY OF CONGRESS CATALOG CARD NUMBER: 78-120657

TO

MY MOTHER
AND FATHER

❁

PREFACE

JAMES'S development as a critic and the special character of his best work are of course the chief matters of
concern in this essay, but they are not the only ones, or
even always the most important. For not only in the prefaces, which are indispensable to an intelligent reader of
James, but throughout the criticism, James's ruling convictions about life and literature are quite evident; and an
effort is here made to examine and weigh these convictions
as carefully as possible. Fiction, criticism, and prefaces,
all point to an intensely self-conscious mind and to a
striking unity of temperament. James is everywhere in
character, and we find in the criticism not merely an aspect
but pretty much the whole man. It offers frequently the
most explicit evidence of temperamental bias, of inclina-
tion and design, of motives and values which dominated
James's whole activity in literature. The "figure in the
carpet" can be discerned, I believe, more readily in his
criticism than in the stories themselves, even in a single
essay, perhaps, like the one on de Maupassant. Apart
from the pleasure of mystification there is no reason to
regard the "figure" as something esoteric, consecrate, and
endlessly debatable.

But I do not wish to suggest, after all, that the main
interest of the criticism and the prefaces lies in something
ulterior. As a body of artistic doctrine the prefaces are
profoundly illuminating, to the general reader as well as
to the admirer of James. "The Art of Fiction" answers
once for all the innumerable dreary manuals for the ama-

teur story-writer, and the drearier "courses" in schools and colleges by which this innocent is beguiled. Further, as to certain writers, James has surely come very near to saying the last word. Taken as a whole his best criticism cannot be matched in English for certain qualities of style, or for the just and vivid communication of literary quality. And the manner in which his taste freed itself from early prepossessions — or, if one likes, the way in which it failed to do so — is highly instructive. As a critic James himself constitutes a "case" of exceptional interest and complexity.

Despite obvious disadvantages it has seemed best on the whole to follow a chronological plan in this essay. But I have tried to keep the plan from interfering with a more or less total view of the subject, especially in the earlier part, where a discussion of James's reviews derives its point mainly from a contrast with his mature criticism. Thus the course of the argument in the first chapter might have been more direct, but not, I believe, without a loss of perspective.

My best thanks are due to Professor Bliss Perry for wise counsel and unfailing kindness, in this as in other matters. I owe thanks to Professor Karl Young for initial encouragement, and to my friend Mr. Roberts Tapley for extremely helpful criticism. Acknowledgment is due to Messrs. Scribner's Sons for their kind permission to quote from James's prefaces and *Notes on Novelists*.

M. R.

CAMBRIDGE, MASSACHUSETTS
June, 1929

CONTENTS

CHAPTER ONE

EARLY REVIEWS

I am of my nature and by the effect of my
own "preoccupations" a critical, a *non-naïf*,
a questioning, worrying reader . . . . . .
James, *Letters*, ii, 334

EARLY REVIEWS

HENRY JAMES was no less singularly gifted as a critic than as a novelist. It might almost be said that criticism and fiction were for him not two arts but one, and that the same faculty of imaginative penetration served him equally well in both. He is, in a sense peculiarly his own, the most critical of novelists; and on the other hand, one of the most imaginative and observant of critics. What interested him both as novelist and critic was the individual "case." The excellence of his criticism, at its best, lies in its happy delineation of both the man and the book, each by help of the other. His power of characterization, the power of epithet, was of a high order. And the flexibility of his later style enabled him to give precision and relief to the subtlest of his perceptions, to produce a picture rich in detail and flawless in proportion, a marvel of literary craftsmanship, whatever its value as criticism. Moreover, his literary character is all of a piece; it pervaded every relation of his life; and whatever he wrote in the fullness of his power is by its sensibility and extraordinary style stamped forever as his own. "I have to the last point," he writes to a correspondent, "the instinct and the sense for fusions and interrelations, for framing and encircling . . . every part of my stuff in every other . . ." [1] This instinct did not fail him in his criticism; it makes an essay like the one on Balzac in *Notes on Novelists* unlike any other criticism whatever, and as much a work of creative genius as

1. *Letters*, ii, 347.

3

The Wings of the Dove or *The Golden Bowl.* "At the time of La Harpe," writes Flaubert, "they [the critics] were grammarians; at the time of Sainte-Beuve and of Taine they are historians. When will they be artists, only artists, but really artists?" [1] A somewhat rigid young New Englander, who stood in Flaubert's presence not long after this was written, supplied in his own way an answer to this question, in a volume entitled *Notes on Novelists.* We shall try to see how the answer was arrived at.

James's writing career began and ended with criticism. Like other prose writers in this age of periodicals he appeared in print for the first time as a reviewer, with a notice of Senior's *Essays on Fiction* in the *North American Review* for October, 1864. His first story came out in the following year. For the next ten years or so he devoted himself to reviewing and to experiments in fiction. His activity, which was great, appears to have been about equally divided between the two, and his success was more apparent in reviewing than in story-telling. Some of the best of his early reviews have been collected in a volume; in all, they are numerous, and they are to be found for the most part in the New York *Nation*, and occasionally also in the *North American Review,* the *Atlantic Monthly,* and the *Galaxy.* James's term as a reviewer lasted roughly until the publication of his first volume of critical studies, *French Poets and Novelists,* in 1878. All of these studies had appeared previously in various periodicals, the earliest, an article on Gautier, in 1873. We shall therefore consider James's proper work as a critic to have begun in that year, and regard the preceding nine years, from 1864 to 1872, as his period of apprenticeship. The work of these years, the display of a critical talent in the germ, deserves more than a casual glance.

1. *The George Sand–Gustave Flaubert Letters,* New York (1921), p. 121.

4

First of all, there is a meaning in the mere quantity of this journeyman's work, considering that James's ambition after all was to be a novelist and that his stories were finding as ready a market as his reviews. Most writers derive their earliest inspiration from books; but the point here is not so much that James set himself to imitate other writers as that he breathed, almost from infancy, the air of criticism, of detached curiosity, the air of the theatre, the library, and the museum. He had as a youth little contact with the grosser realities of life, and no incentive to action. Apparently the only career he ever contemplated was the career of letters, and he seems to have been as completely indifferent to everything else as it is possible for one to be. He was destined both by nature and by the peculiar circumstances of his upbringing for the part of a spectator of life, obliged only to perceive and understand. In certain respects, the James household provided an excellent medium for the critical side of his genius, a medium in which cosmopolitanism, art, intellectual freedom, a horror of the market-place, humor, and morality were oddly mingled. All these elements left their mark on James's mind. He tells us how as a small boy, listening to the comments of his elders at a performance of "Uncle Tom's Cabin," he "got his first glimpse of the free play of mind over a subject which was to throw him with force at a later stage of culture, when subjects had considerably multiplied, into the critical arms of Matthew Arnold."[1] This free play of mind constituted the greater part of Henry James's participation in life. His curiosity, in certain directions at least, was immense. But from the first it was the curiosity of the observer, mainly intellectual. Even as a small boy, so he records in one of his autobiographical books, he was already aware that "one way of taking life was to go in

1. *A Small Boy and Others*, p. 163.

for everything and everyone, which kept you abundantly occupied, and the other way was to be occupied, quite as occupied just with the sense and image of it all, and on only a fifth of the actual immersion." [1] There is an artistic economy about this, as a philosophy of life, which is characteristic, both of James's strength and of his weakness. The small boy had probably not reasoned the matter out, but we may well believe that he unconsciously acted in this faith. It became at any rate the principle of James's whole life. As a young man he finds his first experience of England a "delightful affair fraught . . . with possibilities of adventure for the mind." [2] At an advanced age he writes to a correspondent, "Let your soul live — it's the only life that isn't, on the whole, a sell." [3] "Reading," he says, "tends to take for me the place of experience — or rather to *become* itself (pour qui sait lire) experience concentrated." [4]

What is the bent of James's early critical genius, with what books and authors does it occupy itself, and on what terms? The answer must be qualified by certain allowances for the conditions of book-reviewing. For example, James's *Nation* reviews have a sharper edge than the others, an air of world-weary sophistication which is in keeping with a touch of smartness in the periodical as a whole. His least pardonable invective, like the attacks on Whitman, Browning, and Swinburne, occurs in his *Nation* reviews. Again, the point may be illustrated by a comparison of two of James's reviews, one of which appeared in the *Galaxy*, with his signature, the other in the *Nation*, anonymously. [5] The subject of the first was Tennyson's "Queen Mary"; of the second, the poet's "Harold." The

---

1. *A Small Boy and Others*, p. 290.   2. *The Middle Years*, p. 15.
3. *Letters*, i, 252.   4. *Ibid.*, ii, 11.
5. Both are reprinted in *Views and Reviews*, compiled by Le Roy Phillips, Boston, 1908.

difference between these two plays is certainly not great; but while James's review of the earlier work is an admirable piece of criticism, full of sympathy and insight, containing some of the best passages in all his earlier work, and above all finely urbane, his treatment of the later play in the *Nation* exhibits some of the worst faults of the junior reviewer; it is flippant, patronizing, and tasteless.

Perhaps the most obvious feature of James's criticism as a whole is its limited range. It is almost exclusively contemporary, and its chief subject-matter is nineteenth-century fiction, English and French. The early reviews exhibit, naturally, a greater variety than the later formal criticism. In a solitary excursion into German literature, the reviewer discusses a translation of *Wilhelm Meister;* [1] he turns to a remote past and writes with sturdy good sense of Epictetus; [2] he devotes considerable attention to poetry and criticism. Nevertheless the reviews display both his limited range and his abiding predilections. More than half deal with novels, and about a third with French writers. Balzac, George Sand, George Eliot, Trollope, Mérimée, Gautier, and Hawthorne are writers to whom James returned, in some instances again and again, in his mature critical studies. His saturation in French literature began in his boyhood with a passionate devotion to George Sand and the *Revue des Deux Mondes.* Mérimée was his first literary model. The example of Balzac inspired his attempt at local color in *Roderick Hudson.* [3] Balzac is described in one of the reviews as "the novelist who of all novelists was certainly most of one"; [4] and the observation lies at the very heart of James's later criticism of Balzac. To the

1. *Notes and Reviews*, Cambridge, Massachusetts, 1921.
2. *Ibid.*
3. *Novels and Tales*, New York ed., vol. i, preface.
4. Review, "Historical Novels," *Nation*, New York, August 15, 1867.

young reviewer George Sand seemed the perfect novelist, the unique example of a woman with a "first-class imagination," her *Le Dernier Amour* was the last word in narrative art, and her style immeasurably superior to that of Dickens and Thackeray.[1] Another of his early admirations, a good deal qualified, was George Eliot, whose English decorum and moral interest gave her in the end an immense advantage over her French rivals in James's estimation. "It was by George Eliot's name," he writes, referring to this early period, "that I was to go on knowing, was never to cease to know, a great treasure of beauty and humanity, of applied and achieved art."[2] She is the subject of his first extended article, and of one of the most mellow and inspired of the later studies. But the name which recurs oftenest in the reviews is that of Trollope, towards whom the reviewer exhibits a strong antipathy, at once surprising and enlightening. For nothing shows so well the growth of James's insight as a comparison of this early criticism of Trollope with the finely appreciative and eloquent essay in *Partial Portraits*, and nothing at the same time is more characteristic of James's whole critical approach than the grounds of his disapproval of Trollope. Other and more violent antipathies were Swinburne, Victor Hugo, and Walt Whitman. At twenty-two, James was an uncompromising foe of novelty and expansiveness in literature, though many years afterwards he could admire the freshness of Kipling and the "incomparable cheek" of H. G. Wells. When, writing of Hugo in 1874, he says of himself, "We confess to a conservative taste in literary matters — to a relish for brevity, for conciseness, for elegance, for perfection of form,"[3] he is describing a preference which dominated his

1. Review of George Sand's *Mlle. Merquem*, *Nation*, July 30, 1868.
2. *The Middle Years*, p. 62.
3. Review of Hugo's *Ninety-Three*, *Nation*, April 9, 1874.

literary taste to the end. The contrast is great between the trenchant and often superficial conclusions of the reviews and the half-lights, the interfusions and subtleties of James's latest criticism, yet even more striking perhaps is a similarity within this contrast, a persistence of inherited ideas, a certain moral coloring which is to a large degree unaffected by an immense progress in esthetic perception. It is apparent from the start that we are dealing with a thoroughly self-conscious mind. James's reviews leave us in no doubt as to the principles upon which their judgments are based. Moreover, the principles are numerous and final; the reviewer had supplied himself with a complete philosophy of criticism, and indeed of everything else, as is the way of reviewers. When he therefore encounters a mind like Sainte-Beuve's,[1] apparently unequipped with ultimate views, he is quick to recognize a fault. The French critic does not take life seriously enough. "After all his experience," remarks James, with an early New England sternness, "Sainte-Beuve ought to be more melancholy." Besides, he is "little of a moralist" and not "overmuch of a thinker";[2] in a word, he is deficient in principles and general ideas. There are two types of critic, the reviewer points out, great and small, philosopher and historian, master of general principles and student of detail. Goethe is an example of the philosophical critic. Sainte-Beuve is the historian, but even as an historian he is very one-sided, for his history is without perspective, its scale is too small; he does not take sufficiently extensive views. Worst of all in Sainte-Beuve is what James calls the "servility of his mind," the quality which Scherer had admiringly described as "un liquide transparent qui, versé successivement dans plusieurs vases, prend la forme et réfléchit

1. *Notes and Reviews*, "A French Critic," p. 103.
2. Review of Sainte-Beuve, *Nation*, June 4, 1868.

9

la couleur de tous." [1] Sainte-Beuve then, being neither a
moralist nor a thinker, and only partially an historian, is
not in the reviewer's opinion a true critic at all. He is only
a psychologist and a writer, and all his merits are nothing
but a "passion for literature and a gift of expression."
Truly, these might have seemed enough even to a young
reviewer, though not perhaps to the son of a Swedenbor-
gian philosopher, bred in an air of conscious culture and
"ideas." But not many years after the review was written
James completely reversed his judgment, and recognized
a great critical virtue in the "servility" of Sainte-Beuve's
mind. His later opinion is summed up in the statement,
"the measure of my enjoyment of a critic is the extent to
which he resembles Sainte-Beuve." [2] What the reviewer
says of Sainte-Beuve is almost exactly what he might
have said of his own later criticism, had he had the privilege of reviewing it. He would have been prompt to call
attention to its lack of general ideas, as the young critic
at least understood the term, and to its circumscribed
range, and he could hardly have described himself otherwise or better than as a psychologist and writer, whose
chief, if not his only, merits were a passion, rather narrow,
for literature and a gift of expression, concluding there-
from that true criticism was not in him.

Estimates of other critics are in the same vein as that of
Sainte-Beuve. A review of Swinburne [3] may be cited,
though it came a little after the period we are considering.
Again the gist of the reviewer's opinion is that Swinburne's
essays are not true criticism. They are only "splendid
imaginative comment." Swinburne, it is true, has poetic

1. Edmond Scherer, *La Littérature Contemporaine*, i, 345.
2. Review, "Matthew Arnold," *English Illustrated Magazine*, January,
1884.
3. *Views and Reviews.*

insight, imagination, sensibility; he is profoundly right about Arnold's poetry and about Byron's; but his qualities are fatally overbalanced by his "inordinate sense of the picturesque" and his attempt "to make lurid imagery do duty as thought," by his total inability to understand human nature, and most of all by his poverty of thought and moral insight. It is hardly necessary to point out that there is a measure of truth in this judgment, as there is in the one of Sainte-Beuve. Both, like many others in the reviews, are based upon sound observation, which fails to bear fruit because the emphasis and proportion are wrong in the criticism as a whole. The critic is too intent upon the defects of his subject's qualities, too much absorbed in his own point of view, and indifferent to the possible uses of the imagination. He resents surprises, like many of his brothers in the craft. James's preconceptions, in other words, did not prevent him from seeing, but they did prevent him from putting a right interpretation upon what he saw. It might be added, moreover, that he did not, as is proved by his own later criticism, altogether understand his early principles or know how to use them. Criticism according to rules is a necessary thing, there being in a sense no other kind; everything depends upon the rules and upon the intelligence with which they are applied. It is the critic's business to know what to look for; he cannot know too well, for he must be prepared to recognize excellence in a thousand guises. In so far as James was led astray, it was not by a theory of criticism so much as by the partial and rigid application of a theory.

The results of this application were not always negative. In two of the critics who came under his notice, Matthew Arnold and Edmond Scherer, James found what he was looking for, a methodical, thoroughly intellectualized, and morally significant criticism. In Arnold there is a drawback.[1] For the latter's strongest quality is, after all, to the reviewer's mind, not reason but feeling or sensibility. Is the critic more called upon to feel or to understand, James asks himself, and the answer is of course, that reason ought to come first, that is to say, general principles are more important than a perception of individual quality. This is precisely the dictum which James ardently denounced in his later criticism, pleading always for a finer perception on the critic's part, a livelier receptiveness, a greater openness to impressions. But if reason is not quite the chief of Arnold's qualities, it is nevertheless prominent among them. He had what the reviewer quaintly terms "science" and "logic," two of the highest attributes of a critic, and the equivalent of reason.

But the critic who comes off best in the reviews is Scherer.[2] Unlike Sainte-Beuve he had, to begin with, an explicit philosophy. More than that, his philosophy suited the reviewer perfectly, so perfectly that he made it his own. Here at last were the solid moral interest and the zeal for general truth so little apparent to James in Sainte-Beuve. Yet the most significant ground of the reviewer's admiration is the fact that Scherer, for all his interest in morality and general ideas, remains undogmatic. He has ideas, but what is even better is the fact that he does not insist upon them. It is a part of his philosophy not to insist upon them. To James's mind, the great thing about Scherer is that he combines intellectual freedom, as well as a passion for freedom of every kind, with a sense of responsibility to a kind of ultimate social truth, the product of partial and individual truths, which is always growing and changing, and can only be arrived at gradually by trial and

1. *Views and Reviews.*
2. *Notes and Reviews.* Compare a later and much less flattering review of Scherer in the *Nation* for April 6, 1876.

error, by experience, of which freedom to think and act is of course an indispensable condition. Scherer is a pragmatist. If heretofore James's temper has seemed dogmatic — as indeed it was — we must now recognize a pull in the opposite direction, towards the free play of mind which he admired in Arnold, and the sceptical, inquiring, tentative philosophy of Scherer. The point is that Scherer was moralist, liberal, and man of the world. It was the ideal combination. It proved that one could be European, could be in the widest sense a man of taste and experience and still remain intellectually and morally respectable, according to the best standards of Henry James, Senior, and his friends. One could submit to and welcome a thorough discipline of mind and conscience, yet scorn the "flagrant morality" of the meeting-house and the depressing standards of the market-place. One could be at once a man and an artist, without a taint of provincialism, quite enlightened and cosmopolitan, retaining in the service of beauty, of taste, and irony, all the moral and intellectual faculties of a saint and philosopher.

The reviewer's philosophy is summed up in his own profession of critical faith.[1] His first duty he felt was to detach from the work "any ideas or principles appreciable and available to the cultivated public judgment." He will care "only in a minor degree whether his relation to a work is one of praise or blame," the important thing being not the failure or success of a particular book, but the lessons involved in either, the underlying principle and ultimate law of art. His function is a grave and comprehensive one. He is at once a philosopher, moralist, and historian, for it is obvious that he cannot hope to discover the ultimate grounds of taste without a wide knowledge of men and things. And, in accordance with Scherer's view, it is his

1. Review, "Modern Women," *Nation*, October 22, 1868.

duty to be an intellectual explorer and to contribute to the world's sum of ideas. He must be at the same time very critical of the claims of other explorers, an injunction much easier to observe than the preceding one, as the reviewer's practice shows. If he cannot add anything new, he can at least preserve the old; he can be a bulwark of tradition and a guardian of taste; he can challenge literary novelty with the logic of perfection and the experience of the past. In a word, the critic's function is to expound the philosophy of art, to guide public taste, and to enlighten the erring author. To this end he must be "before all things, clear and emphatic."

Thus baldly summarized, the theory may seem a little fatuous, and the reviews are never that, but only as a rule a little too sure of their ground. Again, it is a question of manipulation rather than of principles. Nowhere, for example, is a principle or idea available to the cultivated public judgment more skillfully conveyed than in some of James's latest and best criticism, and the difference between it and the reviews is simply the difference between success and failure. And in the prefaces, James has added a good deal to the world's sum of ideas about art. Nor with all his profound absorption in the metaphysics of art did he ever cease to be a moralist. Yet the differences, on the surface at least, could hardly be more striking. So far from wishing to be clear and emphatic, the later James assures us that he "likes ambiguities and detests great glares, preferring thus for [his] critical progress no less than for [his] pedestrian progress the cool and shade to the sun and dust of the way." [1] He insists that "criticism in the nobler sense of the word is for me enjoyment," [2] that the critical principle is the "appreciative, the *real* gustatory." [3] He is the

1. *Notes of a Son and Brother*, p. 106.
2. *Letters*, i, 396.   3. *Ibid.*, ii, 137.

critic, he tells us, "for whom the happy accident of character, whatever form it may take, is more of a bribe to interest
than the promise of some character cherished in theory —
the appearance of justifying some foregone conclusion as to
what a writer or a book 'ought,' in the Ruskinian sense, to
be; the critic in a word, who has, *a priori*, no rule for a
literary production but that it shall have genuine life";
who "likes a writer exactly in proportion as he is a challenge, an appeal to interpretation, intelligence, ingenuity,
to what is elastic in the critical mind." [1]

This might be a direct comment upon his own early
reviews. The difference may seem to be merely a difference
in critical manners, but it goes in fact much deeper than
that. The emphasis in the later view is all upon acuteness
of perception and openness to impressions, upon enjoyment, and the discernment of values, the first of which
values, the indispensable one, is "genuine life." In this one
requisite, more is implied really than in nearly all the *a
priori* standards of the reviews taken together. But James
by no means abandoned certain of the basic criteria here
and there so ineptly handled in the reviews. He multiplied distinctions, he refined and qualified, he perfected
his grasp and learned — which is the secret of the whole
matter — how to apply his standards with a deftness and
tact quite foreign to the reviews. Much that was characteristic of James to the end is present in this early work:
certain predominant interests, an Anglo-Saxon tenderness
of mind; but of the particular turn of his critical genius,
at least as we have it in *Notes on Novelists*, of the instinct
for interfusions and relations, of the power of penetrating
and absorbing a subject, we have not so much as a hint.
James's starting point both in criticism and fiction was a
long way from his goal. If we assume that his development

1. *Views and Reviews*, pp. 227–228.

was natural and that his latest writing, like *The Ambas-sadors*, and *Notes on Novelists*, is the best expression of his genius, we must conclude that he was unusually slow to achieve a characteristic form. The autobiographical books are in this respect misleading, for with his later intensely subjective habit of mind, James interpreted his past wholly in terms of his present, transmuting the small boy into the man of sixty, rubbing a magic sponge over the page of his early life and reading an ideal story between the lines, a story which often contradicts the plain text. For example, we find him in *The Middle Years* writing of his early admi-ration for George Eliot and describing how he had "re-joiced without reserve" in *Felix Holt* when the book first came out,[1] about fifty years before, when James's career as a reviewer was just beginning. Now if we turn to the con-temporary record of this "rejoicing," that is, to James's review of *Felix Holt*,[2] we find indeed much that is compli-mentary, but we find its main conclusion to be nevertheless that the book stamps George Eliot as a "secondary thinker and incomplete artist."

There is a theory of fiction in the reviews, having a no-ticeable though far-off and somewhat distorted resemblance to "The Art of Fiction" and the prefaces. The reviewer busily gathers the lessons of success and failure, mostly the latter, with a noble indifference to the fate of authors and with an uncommon aptitude for pointing the moral, though by no means without humor and good sense. But the moral, though often sound enough in itself, is perhaps just as often irrelevant or misapplied and strikes one as out of relation to the subject, as having been evolved in a vacuum instead of being steeped in the qualities of the book or writer under review. It is applied from without instead of

1. *The Middle Years*, p. 63.
2. *Notes and Reviews*.

issuing from the deepest and most significant part of the subject itself. Thus we are told that the primary function of a book is to suggest thought, and from this we are to conclude that Trollope is not worth reading.[1] The premise may be true, but not the conclusion surely. Again, the great novelist, we are told, must be a philosopher and know *man* as well as *men*, for without such knowledge there is no great art. This is true, yet the disparagement of Dickens[2] which follows from it in the reviews is irrelevant. Not that either generalization is wholly inapplicable. It is fair to say that neither Trollope nor Dickens is profound as Shakespeare and Goethe are, but when that has been said, when we have been told what Trollope and Dickens are not, we still wait to be told what they are. Of literature as of criticism the reviewer demands general ideas and great truths. Graces of form, humor, observation, eloquence, are not enough. He dwells upon the intellectual limitations of Stoicism,[3] upon the complete absence of thought in the letters of Eugénie de Guérin,[4] upon the fact that Madame de Sévigné, despite her perfect style, is "not often tempted to utter very composite truths."[5] Gautier is a spiritual bankrupt, who has neither mind nor soul, but only a wonderful eye for the picturesque.[6] Ruskin wanders in a world of "unreason and illusion."[7] Trollope's *Belton Estate*[8] is "without a single idea and incompetent to the primary function of a book — to suggest thought." John Grey, in Trollope's *Can You Forgive Her?*[9] proves that the

1. See *Notes and Reviews, passim,* for the several reviews of Trollope discussed here.
2. *Views and Reviews.* James's opinion of Dickens never altered much. See *Letters,* ii, 40.
3. *Notes and Reviews,* "Epictetus."
4. *Ibid.,* "Eugénie de Guérin's Letters."
5. *Ibid.*
6. Review of Gautier's *Tableaux de Siège, Nation,* January 25, 1872.
7. *Letters,* i, 20.   8. *Notes and Reviews.*   9. *Ibid.*

writer is "simply unable to depict a *mind* in any liberal sense of the word." Most of these observations lie at the centre of the reviewer's whole estimate of his subject. But the best example is the well-known review of Whitman. This is how, he fancies, the Spirit of Intelligence would speak to the poet:

> We look in vain, however, through your book for a single idea. We find nothing but flashy imitations of ideas. We find a medley of extravagances and commonplaces. We find art, measure, grace, sense sneered at on every page and nothing positive given in their stead. To be positive, one must have something to say; to be positive requires reason, labor, and art; and art requires above all things a suppression of one's self to an idea. . . . You must respect the public which you address; for it has taste if you have not. . . . It is not enough to be rude, lugubrious, and grim. You must also be serious. You must forget yourself in your ideas. Your personal qualities — the vigor of your temperament, the manly independence of your nature, the tenderness of your heart — these facts are impertinent.[1]

In much the same spirit he reproaches Trollope for dealing in "small effects," for contenting himself with a trivial subject-matter. Trollope is an excellent observer, yes, but "Why," asks James, "doesn't he observe great things as well as little ones?" What the reviewer has specifically in mind as a little thing is Mrs. Mackenzie's dinner-party in Trollope's *Miss Mackenzie*.[2] The episode is a masterly blending of the humor and pathos of the shabby-genteel, and is the best thing in the book. Balzac himself has few things of the kind that are better. But to the reviewer, who made a god of Balzac, the episode seemed uninteresting and unimportant. It was not worth doing. He grants that it is admirably faithful, clever, successful, but to

1. *Views and Reviews*, p. 108. Originally published in the *Nation* of November 16, 1865.
2. *Notes and Reviews*.

what, he asks, is it faithful, and in what does it succeed? For that is the test question about a work of art. And for that very reason, James might have been more careful to answer it correctly. "It is perhaps well," he writes, "that we should learn how superficial, how spiritless, how literal human feeling can become, but is a novel here our proper lesson-book?" It is true that a novel's "foremost claim to merit, and indeed the fullest measure of its merit, is its *truth*." But, the reviewer argues, it must be truth in a large and commanding sense. "To be completely great," he says, "a work of art must lift up the heart."[1] Trollope may be true to common life, but he is not true to human nature; he ignores the ideal; his characters are but "the halves of men and women," without passion, nobility or idealism, and instead of "reflecting life upon the details, borrow it from them, and so borrow the contagion of death." In a word, Trollope is a sordid and unimaginative realist. In the same way, Dickens, despite his humor and observation, is merely the greatest of superficial novelists, for he too lacks insight, philosophy, the ability to see deep into the human heart and to treat a great passion seriously. True, he reconciles us to the commonplace and to the odd, but to the reviewer this seems a questionable service. The same deficiency of imagination may be observed in George Eliot[2] also. She has more of the precious quality than Trollope,— she could not possibly have less, — but the quantity is not much after all, as may be seen by comparing Hetty Sorel's flight with the escape of the heroine in *Jane Eyre*. George Eliot, like Trollope, like Dickens, is a good observer, but of what use, asks the reviewer, is her "microscopic observation, not a myriad of whose keen notations are worth a single one of those great sympathetic guesses with which a

1. *Notes and Reviews*, "The Last French Novel."
2. *Ibid.*, "Felix Holt."

real master attacks the truth?" For, "to write a novel," he observes truly, "it is not necessary to have been a traveller, an adventurer, a sight-seer; it is simply necessary to be an artist." [1] The basis of all imaginative writing is a "compromise with reality." This is as true of the novel as of the romance, the only difference being that the romance carries the compromise much further than the novel. "A good ghost story," remarks James, foreshadowing the brilliant technique of *The Turn of the Screw*, "a good ghost story . . . must be connected at a hundred points with the common objects of life." [2]

Again, the unimaginative realist's absorption in detail results in the frequent absence of form in his work. This is noticeably true of George Eliot. Her novels, excepting only *Silas Marner*, lack structure, composition, and drama. This is what stamps her as a "secondary thinker and incomplete artist." Her plots are diffuse, artificial, and dramatically weak; and the reviewer concludes that it is "neither in her conceptions nor in her composition that George Eliot is strongest; it is in her *touches*." [3] This is the mark of the inferior artist, for "the soul of a novel," asserts the reviewer, "is its action"; [4] the strength of a story lies in the story itself, not in any incidental embellishments, such as local color. Every word in a story which is not in effect narrative, which does not advance the story, is simply irrelevant. The perfect novel, in other words, is all narration; [5] the imperfect one is a compound, not of narration and description, but of narration and superfluities. The young critic's insistence upon a severe discipline of form had a crusading ardor about it,

1. *Notes and Reviews*, "The Noble School of Fiction."
2. *Ibid.*, "Miss Braddon."
3. *Views and Reviews*, "The Novels of George Eliot."
4. *Notes and Reviews*, "Azarian."   5. *Ibid.*

for the literary fashion of the time, in America at least, demanded what he calls the "research of local colors," painting as contrasted with drawing, "touches" as opposed to composition and design. It was the age of the lady novelist. "If women," remarks James, "are unable to draw, they can . . . paint, and this is what realism requires." [1] But the realism so produced is a false realism. The true article is not a piling up of details which obscure design in the work as a whole; its secret is a complete expressiveness, such as Balzac achieves. [2]

These conclusions, though perhaps of no great interest in themselves, are valuable to the student of James because, while resembling it so little in form and critical value, they yet reflect so much of the groundwork of temperament in the later criticism. Like the estimate of Sainte-Beuve, they are a mixture of the true and false, the mingling of a capacity for generalizing with a frequent perversity of judgment. The reviewer's statements are too often absolute when they should be relative, and he shows little of the delicate faculty of insinuating reserves, of fixing both a quality and its defect at one stroke, which, when the subject is a worthy one, is the perfection of good manners and sound method in criticism. But the reviewer's subject we must remember was often neither worthy nor of his own choice. Again, like the view of Sainte-Beuve, James's opinion of Trollope underwent a complete change, [3] and that of George Eliot was greatly modified. Thus, in the essay in *Partial Portraits*, Trollope is cited as an example of the wholesome exercise of imagination, and what seemed to the reviewer his main fault becomes for the critic his

1. *Notes and Reviews*, "The Schönberg-Cotta Family."
2. *Ibid.*, "Azarian."
3. As early as 1868. See the review of *Linda Tressel* in the *Nation* for April 6, 1868.

21

main virtue. "His inestimable merit," writes James, "was a complete appreciation of the usual." A significant comparison in the essay explains this change, in part at least, and shows just how far it went. After pointing out that Trollope has imagination, James adds that it is moreover imagination of a peculiarly healthful and refreshing kind, sensitive in the moral sphere, and soundly English, the kind of imagination precisely whose absence in the work of the French naturalists, of Flaubert, Zola, and the de Goncourts, vitiates all their product. Compared with these latter, Trollope was sheer poetry. With what grateful ardor James dwells upon the superior humanity of the English novel as compared with the French. His fondness for England and things English was greatly deepened during his year in Paris. If America was not his spiritual home, France was even less so; and though he haunted Flaubert's circle and learned from it doubtless many things about art, not least of the things he learned there was how to value George Eliot. But if the application in the later criticism is different from that of the reviews, the principle is the same. Both the impatience with Trollope's realism and the later quarrel with French naturalism sprang from the same quality of mind in the critic — an idealism, a faith in the discipline of mind and conscience, shading off into the romantic. James learned more and more how to keep his scruples in their place, how to give rein to his taste, to his matchless feeling for quality; he refined upon his scruples, but he never abandoned them.

And yet from the first, under the powerful influence of Balzac,[1] his conscious bent in literature was toward the realistic. His objection to Trollope was only of course an objection to realism gone wrong, inadequate to its highest

1. "... to be real in writing [as Balzac was real] is to express ..." *Notes and Reviews*, "Azarian."

function, that of interpreting the life of the spirit. When he wrote, "Let your soul live — it's the only life that isn't, on the whole, a sell," he was saying what he had always felt to be true; and the statement reflects an early, instinctive wisdom. No literature that failed to do justice to it could satisfy Henry James. To the reviewer, Trollope's characters seemed but the halves of men and women, without passion, nobility, or idealism, just as, to the author of *Notes on Novelists*, D'Annunzio's fatal weakness was the moral and intellectual insufficiency of his characters. What repelled him in both cases was the absence of a capacity to "vibrate," to feel experience as James himself felt it.

Such a capacity, in the degree in which James possessed it, and accompanied by James's fastidiousness, is prone to modify experience in the interest of good taste, of purity and grace, in the interest above all of beauty, and to mould it even beyond recognition or to ignore experience altogether. Thus he admits of some of the stories of his early and middle periods that he had been led to romanticize by what he calls his "incurable preference for grace." [1] Some of the realities he dealt with later on as a story-teller are dark and cynical enough and present human nature in anything but a rosy light. But however dark the evil may be, it never appears gross; in a sense, indeed, it may be said never to appear at all, for its remote spiritual vibrations, the nobility, courage, intelligence, which the concrete evil in one way or another gives rise to, are all that figure in the story. The avoidance of grossness is almost the whole of James's morality. The reviewer is emphatic in the assertion that art is not moral instruction; he despises the novel which teaches a lesson. "Of a genuine novel," he observes, "the meaning and the lesson are infinite"; they

1. See *Novels and Tales*, xv, Preface, p. xviii.

should not be "narrowed down to a special precept." [1] The measure of a novel's merit is "its *truth* — its truth to something, however questionable that thing may be in point of morals," [2] for "intelligent realism, in art, carries with it its own morality." [3] It is a mistake to prohibit anything which "makes a claim to artistic merit." [4] The artist must be free; his choice of subject is his own affair. But the subject is nevertheless the supreme test of an artist's value, because it is a test of the reach of his perception and so of his moral quality. This is the ultimate doctrine of the reviews and of James's criticism as a whole.

In no respect do the reviews anticipate the later James more clearly than in their attention to form. The reviewer was ruled by a high and for the most part exceptionally intelligent faith in the discipline of art, of craftsmanship and design. He had begun to learn the lesson of form as a child, during his family's European pilgrimages, from his contact with Parisian art and French fiction. The refrain of Paris in the child's ear was, he tells us, "art, art, little pilgrims, learn what *that* is." [5] The lesson was a rather conventional one, the conception of art was formal and restricted, more French than English, nearer to classic than to romantic French taste. It was hampered by James's constitutional preference for grace, in poetry especially. He never had the catholicity of taste which marks the great critic, for the simple reason that his interests were few. He was neither the heir of all the ages nor ever quite in step with his own age. He was of the immediate past, most at home with the "tender grace of a day that is dead," to employ

1. *Notes and Reviews*, "The Schönberg-Cotta Family."
2. *Ibid.*, "Azarian."
3. Review of Gustave Droz's *Autour d'une Source*, *Atlantic Monthly*, August, 1871.
4. Review of Feydau's *Les Moeurs du Jour*, *Nation*, January 23, 1868.
5. *A Small Boy and Others*, p. 338.

one of his favorite quotations, a day near enough to be remembered, but not intrusively, not harshly present. Very significant is the observation in his earliest review[1] that the novelist is "saved" by work, by the effort, that is, to surmount technical difficulties, and it is from the same point of view that he alludes many years later to the "fluid puddings" which pass for novels with the admirers of Tolstoy and Dostoieffsky. He condemns the want of design in Swinburne's *Chastelhard*,[2] saying, "It is easy to write energetic poetry, but very difficult to write a good play." This sense of the difficulty of writing a good play is surely one of the reasons why James persisted in his unhappy experiments in play-writing. The form, with its exacting demand on a gift for design, was a challenge, an irresistible lure. And the spirit in which it should be met, the spirit which was later to give birth to such miracles of technique as *What Maisie Knew*, is finely expressed by James as early as 1875, in this highly characteristic passage:

The fine thing in a real drama, generally speaking, is that, more than any other work of literary art, it needs a masterly structure. It needs to be shaped and fashioned and laid together, and this process makes a demand upon an artist's rarest gifts. He must combine and arrange, interpolate and eliminate, play the joiner with the most attentive skill; and yet at the end effectually bury his tools and his sawdust, and invest his elaborate skeleton with the smoothest and most polished integument. The five-act drama — serious or humorous, poetic or prosaic — is like a box of fixed dimensions and inelastic material, into which a mass of precious things are to be packed away. It is a problem in ingenuity and a problem of the most interesting kind. The precious things in question seem out of all proportion to the compass of the receptacle; but the artist has an assurance that with patience and skill a place may be made for each, and that nothing

1. *Notes and Reviews*, "Fiction and Sir Walter Scott."
2. *Ibid.* Compare James Russell Lowell's review of the play to much the same effect in the *North American Review*, April, 1866.

25

need be clipped or crumpled, squeezed or damaged. The false dramatist either knocks out the sides of his box, or plays the deuce with the contents; the real one gets down on his knee, disposes of his goods, tentatively, this, that, and the other way, loses his temper, but keeps his ideal, and at last rises in triumph, having packed his coffer in the one way that is mathematically right. It closes perfectly and the lock turns with a click; between one object and another you cannot insert the point of a penknife.[1]

On a good many points then, concerning the art of fiction, the only difference between the reviews and James's mature criticism is the superior felicity of expression in the latter. That it is more important for a writer to be an artist than to have had a wide experience of life is an idea conspicuous both in "The Art of Fiction," and in the prefaces. So too are the conception of the novel as a personal impression of life,[2] the definition of romance, the refusal to take very seriously a distinction between realistic and romantic, the demand for the ideal, the insistence upon form and upon freedom for the artist. Where the reviewer's native shrewdness was helped by his own practice of fiction and by the liberalizing effect of his acquaintance with French literature, his insight is extraordinarily mature. Nor, as the following excerpt shows, is his grasp by any means confined to technical matters.

It is very common now-a-days for young novelists to build up figures *minus* the soul. There are two ways of so eliminating the spiritual principle. One is by effectually diluting it in the description of outward objects, as is the case with the picturesque school of writing; another is by diluting it in the description of internal subjects. This latter course has been pursued in the volume be-

---

1. *Views and Reviews*, pp. 181, 182. James's admiration for the dramatic form declined after the failure of his experiments in playwriting, 1889–1894.

2. "... he [Trollope] repeats in literature the image projected by life upon his moral consciousness." Review of *Linda Tressel*, *Nation*, June 18, 1868.

fore us. In either case the temperament is the nearest approach we have to a soul.

* * * * * * * * *

There is hardly a page in which the author does not insinuate her conviction that, in proportion as a person is finely organized, in so far is he apt to be the slave of his instincts, — the subject of unaccountable attractions and repulsions, loathings and yearnings.[1]

He can be as occasion demands pleasantly or aggressively satirical.

The chief figure in Miss Winfred Bertram's world, and one quite overshadowing this young lady, is a certain Grace Leigh, who, albeit of a very tender age, is frequently made the mouthpiece of the author's religious convictions and views of life. She is so free from human imperfections, and under all circumstances gravitates so infallibly and gracefully towards the right, that her attitude on any question may almost be taken to settle that question for spirits less clearly illumined. She administers a quiet snub to "Sunday books" by declaring that she possesses none. "I do not think Shakespeare is quite one," she adds, "nor Homer, although it often helps me on Sundays, and every day, to think of them."[2]

We are informed that they [the characters in Charles Kingsley's novels] have "great souls," which on small provocation rush into their eyes and into the grasp of their hands; and they are forever addressing each other as "old boy" and "old girl." "Is *this* ambition?" Has the language of friendship and love no finer terms than these? Those who use them, we are reminded, are gentlemen in the rough. There is, in our opinion, no such thing as a gentleman in the rough. A gentleman is born of his polish.[3]

He is often admirably sane and just, quick to discern affectation and artistic slovenliness, sensitive to ideas, and engagingly free from cant. The writing has a transparent

1. *Notes and Reviews*, "Emily Chester: A Novel," pp. 42, 43.
2. *Ibid.*, "Winifred Bertram," p. 146.
3. *Ibid.*, "The Noble School of Fiction," p. 65.

vigor, verging on the rhetorical; it is lively and pointed; it is youthfully sententious and delights in epigram. And despite the frequent similarity of ideas, it would have taken a truly prophetic insight to recognize in the reviews any promise of the prolonged and winding graces of thought in the prefaces. Moreover, the qualities which give James's later criticism its value, a flawless taste, imagination, and above all, the power of manipulating a subject, are still to come.

CHAPTER TWO

FRENCH POETS AND NOVELISTS

With Sainte-Beuve, as with everyone else, [taste] grew more and more flexible with time; it adapted itself and opened new windows and doors. . . . .

. James, *Sainte-Beuve* (1880)

THE ten years after 1873 were among the most productive and important in James's career, as a novelist
particularly; and they have besides, an unusual interest
for his biographer. For it was in 1875, at the age of thirty-
two, that he made the great decision of his life, the decision
to migrate, and after an unsatisfactory year in Paris, fixed
upon London as his permanent home. He worked fever-
ishly during this ten years, mainly of course in fiction, yet
without abandoning criticism or other incidental writing,
of which he managed to produce an imposing quantity.
This, according to his own view, was his real apprenticeship, both in writing and in the absorption of material for
fiction. In criticism the effect is apparent in a growing flexibility of expression. As for fiction, he is perhaps best known
by the novels and stories of this period. *Roderick Hudson*, *The American*, *The Portrait of a Lady*, were produced
at this time or in the years immediately following, as were
also *The Passionate Pilgrim*, *The Madonna of the Future*,
An International Episode, *The Europeans* (a story excluded
from the definitive edition, which should be read in the
light of his disparagement of New England in his life of
Hawthorne), and finally *Daisy Miller*, which for a brief
moment made James a popular writer. Besides this and
other fiction, and two volumes of formal criticism, there is
a quantity of miscellaneous writing which belongs to this
period. It consists of a series of news letters from Paris, of
a mass of unsigned contributions to the New York *Nation*,
book reviews, art criticism, literary and dramatic notices

31

to the number of a hundred or more, and of two volumes of travel sketches, which are a characteristic and valuable part of James's achievement, and point like his art criticism to Gautier and French tradition generally. The literary criticism of the period consists of some twenty essays, most of which were republished in 1878 in James's first volume of criticism, *French Poets and Novelists*. The study of Hawthorne appeared in the following year.

It is convenient to take 1883 as the farther limit of this period. With one exception, the earliest of the essays in *Partial Portraits* (published in 1888) belongs to that year, and the volume itself is the first in which James achieves a real mastery. It holds a central place in his criticism, like that of the *Portrait of a Lady* among his novels. Also by 1883 he had ceased to produce anonymous reviews and notices. The apprenticeship was over. As the earlier period, 1864–73, was one of mere beginnings, so the present is transitional, carrying forward and bringing to a close the work of the earlier years, and breaking new ground in the life of Hawthorne and in the succession of essays which appear in *French Poets and Novelists*. In another sense this new work itself is transitional, uneven, as compared with *Partial Portraits*; it recalls not infrequently the summary judgments and imperfect sympathy of the early reviews, though on the other hand it is not far at times from James's best. Yet there can be no doubt about the advance of critical skill in *Partial Portraits*, even if we make allowance for James's greater natural sympathy with its subject-matter. In the midst of the cross-currents of our present period there lies at least one perfect piece of criticism. This is the finely moulded "Conversation on Daniel Deronda," first published in 1876, and not republished until it appeared twelve years later in *Partial Portraits*, with only a few minor verbal changes.

The labors of the reviewer continued after 1873; and as one might expect the difference is great between these later anonymous reviews and some of the admirable full-length criticism produced at the same time. They appear for the most part in the *Nation*, exhibiting the same limitations, and covering much the same ground as the earlier reviews. Their approach to important writers is a little more tentative, and they do not invoke first principles so often. Written in the intervals of more important work, they are more casual and case-hardened, not so gravely magisterial, but also less fresh and zestful. A considerable number are devoted to books of travel, this being a province in which James himself was acquiring mastery. But some of these later reviews, of Browning, Tennyson, Hugo, Gautier, Swinburne, and Hardy, are quite as acrid and sweeping as the worst of the earlier ones. For example, in the very year in which James published one of the most genial and tactfullly searching of all his criticisms, the "Conversation on Deronda," he described Browning's "Inn-Album" in a review,[1] as an "irritating and displeasing performance," wanton, crude, like a "series of rough notes for a poem," containing not a single poetical phrase, or a line of comprehensible, consecutive statement. And in a review of the following year he dismisses Tennyson's "Harold" as "drama without plot and dialogue without point."[2] He describes Gautier's mind as about on a par with that of an intelligent poodle.[3] He calls Hardy's *Far From the Madding Crowd*[4] a merely clever, superficial imitation of George Eliot; the suspicion that he was dealing with anything more than the average novel of the day never crossed his mind apparently. He complains of its inartistic narrative

1. *Views and Reviews.*   2. *Ibid.*
3. Review of Gautier's *Winter in Russia, Nation,* November 12, 1874.
4. *Nation,* December 24, 1874.

and diffuseness, suggesting that there should be a rule limiting the length of a novel to two hundred pages — this just after he had finished his own *Roderick Hudson*, in two volumes.[1]

But despite irresponsible judgments likes these, the criticism of the period marks an advance which can be easily measured. In 1880 James wrote an article on Sainte-Beuve,[2] and a comparison of this article with the early review shows an interesting change. The reviewer, it will be remembered, objected to Sainte-Beuve's servility of mind, his want of seriousness, his lack of general principles and ideas, insisting upon his limitations in comparison with a philosophical critic like Goethe or Scherer. The critic's emphasis is very different in the article of 1880, in which Sainte-Beuve himself is made a standard of critical excellence. "I take him," says James, "as the very genius of observation, discretion, and taste." In the following words we have at once a description of Sainte-Beuve and the measure of his critic's enlightenment. "The critic of his [Saint-Beuve's] conception was not the narrow lawgiver or the rigid censor that he is often assumed to be; he was the student, the inquirer, the observer, the interpreter, the active, indefatigable commentator, whose constant aim was to arrive at justness of characterization." James writes about his subject in the spirit of these words. Sainte-Beauve's detachment, the free play of his critical intelligence, is for James, as for Matthew Arnold, a value of the highest order. "That," he writes, "is the Sainte-Beuve of my predilection — I may almost say of my faith — the Sainte-Beuve whose judgments had no element of vulgarity, but were always serious, comprehensive, touched

1. The distaste for Hardy seems to have been permanent. See *Letters*, i, 200.

2. *The North American Review*, January, 1880.

with light." Is Sainte-Beuve lacking in general ideas? The critic grants that there is "something feminine in his tact, penetration, subtilty," yet he has also "faculties of the masculine stamp, the solid sense, the constant reason, the copious knowledge, the passion for exactitude, and for general considerations." Is he wanting in moral perception? "Putting aside the imaginative authors, he is the writer," James tells us, "who has imported into literature the largest amount of *life*. No scholar was ever so much of an observer, of a moralist, a psychologist."

The article of 1880 is at once a text and an illustration. James becomes a better critic of Sainte-Beuve by becoming more like his subject, more of an inquirer, observer, and interpreter, whose constant aim is to arrive at justness of characterization. He looks at Sainte-Beuve with the appreciative but none the less appraising eye of the critic who is also an artist and has all the artist's delight in character. He has discovered no new fund of morality or general ideas in Sainte-Beuve; what he has found is a new meaning in the terms themselves, an immense addition of meaning. He has discovered that morality in a writer does not consist in laying down formal precepts, that thought is not confined to the formulation of general principles, that there is both thought and morality in what he calls the importing of life into literature, in psychological truth. And his new flexibility of mind extends to his style and to his whole effort of perception, which ranges freely and impartially, bends with the subject, is always supple, and traces a finely composed and discriminated likeness. He has his eye on the object; he has no motive but a liberal, unhampered curiosity, no desire but to understand; his point of view is implied without a parade of standards; and his observation, so far as it is accurate and revealing, carries its own lesson.

It is unfortunate that the spirit of this article is so frequently absent in *French Poets and Novelists*, where the critic makes painfully short work of Baudelaire and Flaubert, not even deeming the latter worthy of an essay to himself. The essay on Baudelaire had originally appeared in the *Nation* in 1876, and its tone is distinctly that of the hostile reviewer.[1] James makes it the occasion for a sermon on the importance of subject and the puerility of the "art for art" school. He cannot understand why there should have been any fuss about the moral effect of *Les Fleurs du Mal*. It is not a wicked book, it is merely childish. The trouble with Baudelaire is that he tried to be picturesque about a really serious subject, namely, sin. It is all right for Gautier to be picturesque: he neither knows nor pretends to know anything deeper in men and women than the epidermis. But Baudelaire went beyond his depth, and his moral vision, which was dull and immature, simply did not sustain him. His evil is all "rags and bad smells, lurid landscape and unclean furniture," as if, says James derisively, flowers of good were to consist of plum cake and eau de Cologne. If you want to see how childish Baudelaire is, compare him with Hawthorne, to whom, as a New Englander, a true perception of sin was a natural heritage. There are no rags or bad smells in Hawthorne; there is only a kind of purified essence of sin, lying deep in the human consciousness. That is where the true moralist looks for it. Baudelaire and all his contemporaries are prevented from looking by their French superficiality, by what James calls "the Gallic lightness of soil in the moral region." That James's account of Baudelaire is entirely inadequate goes without saying. There is little in the essay about Baudelaire's verse, beyond this brief and reluctant tribute:

1. In this essay, as throughout *French Poets and Novelists*, James's hostility is an echo of conservative French criticism, of Scherer and Brunetière in particular.

Independently of the question of his subjects, the charm of Baudelaire's verse is often of a very high order. He belongs to the class of geniuses in whom we ourselves find but a limited pleasure — laborious, deliberate, economical writers, those who fumble a long time in their pockets before they bring out their hand with a coin in the palm. But the coin when Baudelaire at last produced it was often of a high value. He had an extraordinary verbal instinct and an exquisite felicity of epithet.

The rest is merely an expression of violent distaste, which James shared with most of his contemporaries. The essay tells us more about the critic than about his subject. One feels that James simply recoiled from the lurid landscape and unclean furniture with a wholesome New England disgust, troubling himself little about their meaning or about Beaudelaire's general intention. It is criticism dominated by a refined olfactory sense and an aversion for untidiness and dirt. Incidentally, the critic slips into a profound misunderstanding of Baudelaire's title, *Les Fleurs du Mal*, taking it to mean, not the allurements, but the possible good fruits of evil, a sentimental and ambiguous notion. In a word, he is too preoccupied with Baudelaire's bad smells to try to understand the poet's intention, and the essay reminds us of the review of Walt Whitman.

Its bias is more obstructive than usual, but the disturbing and ever-present sense of a "Gallic lightness of soil in the moral region" is characteristic of *French Poets and Novelists* throughout. It crops out again and again, even in the most sympathetic of the essays. By James himself the attitude was regarded as typically Anglo-Saxon, and he not infrequently alludes to himself in this volume and elsewhere as a spokesman of the English consciousness. It could be sternly aggressive on the side of truth and morals; it shrank, with a touch of spinster-like decorum, from the gross, the vulgar, and the sensual. And perhaps the most important single fact about James is the struggle in him between these reserves and his feeling for art, between his English wholesomeness and his artistic subtlety. His own comment upon a conflict of this kind is interesting.[1] He is speaking of Frank Millet:

> Springing from a very old New England stock, he has found the practice of art a wonderful antidote, in his own language, "for belated Puritanism." He is very modern, in the sense of having tried many things and availed himself of all of the facilities of his time; but especially on this ground of having fought out for himself the battle of the Puritan habit and the aesthetic experiment. His experiment was admirably successful from the moment that the Puritan levity was forced to consent to its becoming a serious one. In other words, if Mr. Millet is artistically interesting to-day (and to the author of these remarks he is highly so) it is because he is a striking example of what the typical American quality can achieve.

It is partly for this reason that James's year in Paris is significant. He went to Paris with the idea of making it his permanent home, and after less than a year's residence, he abandoned the experiment in disgust. A first-hand acquaintance with the literary group consisting of Flaubert, Turgénieff, Zola, the de Goncourts, Daudet, de Maupassant, convinced him that the air they breathed was unhealthy. He had come to Paris because he expected to find there, in his own words, the literary world with which he had the strongest affinity. He was promptly disillusioned. On one side, indeed, his expectation was realized. Contact with the French only deepened his admiration for those things in which they have always excelled, technical curiosity, the exploration of the possibilities of art, critical and self-conscious discussion and experiment. These became more

1. *Picture and Text*, New York, 1893, p. 10.

and more the breath of artistic life to James himself. They were his ties with the French, which nothing could break, and his passionate loyalty to these motives is attested by his whole career, and most strikingly, of course, in one of its last acts, the prefaces to his novels, which for subtle and far-reaching analysis of the technique of an art are unique in English literature. The discussions in Flaubert's salon must have given him much to think about, showing him what it meant to be realistic and to have form, to what lengths a serious concern for art could go, how a supreme sophistication and seriousness in matters of art might be accompanied by what seemed to him an extraordinary moral levity and ignorance of life. He says of the Parisian stage, "I could not but ask myself whether, to become a wholesome and grateful spectacle, even the ugliest possibilities of life need anything more than rigorous exactness of presentation." [1] And some years later, when he is safely established in London, and when his impressions of the French have been softened by time and distance, he makes this comment on an American novel which has just appeared. He is writing from Paris:

I would rather have produced the basest experiment in the "naturalism" that is being practised here than such a piece of six-penny humbug. . . . I have been seeing something of Daudet, Goncourt, Zola; and there is nothing more interesting to me now than the effort and experiment of this little group, with its truly infernal intelligence of art, form, manner — its intense artistic life. They do the only kind of work, to-day, that I respect; and in spite of their ferocious pessimism and their handling of unclean things, they are at least serious and honest. The floods of tepid soap and water which under the name of novels are being vomited forth in England, seem to me, by contrast, to do little honor to our race. [2]

1. "The Parisian Stage," *Nation*, January 9, 1873.
2. *Letters*, i, 104.

But the letters written from Paris during James's actual residence there in 1876 tell a different story. One drawback of a Parisian residence was to be expected. This was the difficulty of establishing "relations," of making oneself at home in a way that would be fruitful to a novelist who wished to observe manners, to portray a social setting. James tried doggedly. He describes how, having no taste whatever for music, he went time after time to a certain French lady's musicales, and stood in a throng near the door during a musical program which lasted for two mortal hours. He might or might not be rewarded on these occasions by a word with Turgénieff. But the sacrifice was unavailing and the whole experiment a failure. He describes his feeling in a letter to William James in 1876:

... my last layers of resistance to a long-encroaching weariness with the French mind and its utterance has fallen from me like a garment. I have done with 'em forever, and am turning English all over. I desire only to feed on English life and the contact of English minds — I wish greatly I knew some. . . . I have got nothing important out of Paris nor am likely to. . . . A good deal of Boulevard and third-rate Americanism: few retributive relations otherwise.[1]

Despite his sympathy with the intense artistic life of the little group gathered at Flaubert's, their aims and preoccupations were in a great measure alien to him. They were realists with absolutely no ideal of delicacy. Grace, charm, purity, refinement, as James understood and prized them, had no place whatever in their scheme of values. They knew the life they described, and James did not, either then or later. He could only marvel at its meanness and brutality. His system of occupying himself only with the sense and image of life, avoiding as much as possible actual immersion, had done little to enable him to understand

1. *Letters*, i, 51.

what Zola and his *confrères* were up to. They were all, in one way or another, men of the world, which James was not. Moreover, they were completely absorbed in their own world, in their own aims, in themselves. It never occurred to them that George Eliot was one of the two greatest living novelists, and they felt no obligation to read her. To James's mind they were intolerably provincial as well as intolerably unclean, and an air of patronage mingles with his contempt, as of one who is at home in countries of the mind, in the discipline of an English conscience, and knows vastly more about human nature than can ever be revealed in a Parisian gutter. Thus, he writes of Flaubert, "I had also the other day, a very pleasant call upon Flaubert, whom I like personally more and more each time I see him. But I think I easily — more than easily — see all round him intellectually." [1] The remark, though not to be taken too seriously perhaps, illustrates nevertheless James's feeling that the French, however mature their sense for form, were in other respects but gifted and perverse children.

Of the whole literary fraternity he writes, "I don't like their wares, and they don't like any others; and besides, they are not *accueillants*. Turgénieff is worth the whole heap of them, and yet he himself swallows them down in a manner that excites my extreme wonder." [2] The French have only one subject. "Novel and drama alike betray an incredibly superficial perception of the moral side of life. It is not only that adultery is their only theme, but that the treatment of it is so monstrously vicious and arid." [3] Of the period in French literature after 1843 he says, "Everything ran to form, and the successful books were apt to resemble little vases, skillfully moulded and chiselled,

1. *Letters*, i, 46.   2. *Ibid.*, p. 49.
3. "The Parisian Stage," *Nation*, January, 1873.

41

into which unclean things have been dropped."[1] He touches upon the evil of literary schools — the school he has in mind is of course Flaubert's, or what was then taken to be Flaubert's, though Flaubert himself disowned it. "French literature abounds in books in which particular tendencies have been pushed to lengths which only a sort of artistic conspiracy of many minds could have reached . . ."[2] He was having too much just then of the French virtue of artistic self-consciousness and experiment. "Zola," he says, "is the most thorough-going of the little band of out and out realists. Unfortunately, the real for him means exclusively the unclean."[3] He approves of the plea in de Goncourt's preface to *La Fille Élisa* for freedom and seriousness on the part of the novelist, but his idea of seriousness differs radically from de Goncourt's, and his objection to *La Fille Élisa* is not that it is serious but that it is intolerably unclean. "Is the history of a prostitute," he asks, "the most serious thing in the list?"[4] One pauses at the question and wonders why the history of a prostitute may not be as serious as that of a respectable woman. What do we mean by seriousness?

What James meant is evident from the essays on Baudelaire and Flaubert. As we have seen, it is to a certain extent the same as the test applied to Trollope in the early reviews. To James, Flaubert was the high priest of Naturalism, the literary father of the de Goncourts, Zola, and de Maupassant, and there was the same corruption in all of them, the same sacrifice of charm, good taste, and morality to a "treacherous ideal." The critic describes this ideal briefly and simply. It was to begin on the outside and to end there. But the real artist is a moralist as well

1. "Charles de Mazada," *Nation*, December 30, 1875.
2. "Parisian Life," *New York Tribune*, February 5, 1876.
3. "Parisian Letter," *New York Tribune*, May 13, 1876.
4. Review of *La Fille Élisa, Nation*, May 10, 1877.

as a painter, and can never be indifferent to the life of the spirit. Flaubert can paint, but he is totally lacking in moral insight. Compared with de Bernard, he is fatally charmless. De Bernard himself is no moralist and remains for that reason "persistently second-rate," but he has gaiety, at least, and urbanity and good taste. He gives pleasure and is to that extent a better novelist than Flaubert. This contrast like a similar one between Baudelaire and Gautier, hits off precisely James's distinction between the French Romantics and their successors. The former were morally immature but good company, the latter were no wiser but less spontaneous in their folly, serious, hard, and disagreeable.

They were ridden by a vicious theory, a theory condemned by its own fruits. *The Temptation of Saint Anthony* is in James's opinion a capital refutation of Flaubert's dogma; its "fatal charmlessness" is "an eloquent plea for the ideal." [1] So too *L'Éducation Sentimentale* is a "laborious monument" to a treacherous theory; there is no more charm in it than there is "perfume in a gravel heap." And it is the most rudimentary of principles that a novel should have "a certain charm." *Madame Bovary* indeed is a masterpiece in its way.

The accumulation of detail is so immense, the vividness of portraiture of people, of places, of times and hours, is so poignant and convincing, that one is dragged into the very current and tissue of the story; the reader himself seems to have lived in it all, more than in any novel we can recall. At the end the intensity of illusion becomes horrible; overwhelmed with disgust and pity he closes the book. [2]

It is "fortunately an inimitable work."

1. Review of *The Temptation of Saint Anthony*, *Nation*, June 4, 1874.
2. *French Poets and Novelists*, p. 262. Compare the contemporary review of *Madame Bovary* in the *Revue des Deux Mondes*, where the point is made that Flaubert does not penetrate to the depths of our moral being.

43

There is perhaps little enough in all this of the efforts of the inquirer and interpreter, little that makes Baudelaire or Flaubert more intelligible to us. James tells us that he holds above everything else to the importance of subject,[1] and ascribes Baudelaire's failure to the fact that he "tried to make fine verses on ignoble subjects." It is the subject that determines the moral quality of a work of art, and this quality is of its very essence, and is inseparable from it. It is

a part of the essential richness of inspiration — it has nothing to do with the artistic process, and it has everything to do with the artistic effect. The more a work of art feels it at its source, the richer it is. . . . People of a large taste prefer rich works . . . and are not inclined to assent to the assumption that the process is the whole work.[2]

The "art for art" doctrine makes this assumption, and is therefore absurd. James dismisses the preface to *Mlle. de Maupin* as puerile. There is a contradiction apparently in the essay on Flaubert, where the critic argues that the novelist should have a distinct moral purpose, as a thing separate from his story, and asserts at the same time that "every out-and-out realist who provokes serious meditation may claim that he is a moralist." But the latter is of course the prevailing doctrine in James.

What then is serious meditation if it is something which neither *Les Fleurs du Mal* nor *L'Éducation Sentimentale* can provoke in the reader? Both works, it may be observed, provoked no little meditation in James himself. What he

1. "I think you are altogether right in returning always to the importance of subject. I hold to this strongly; and if I don't as yet seem to proceed upon it more, it is because, being 'very artistic,' I have a constant impulse to try experiments of form, in which I shall not run the risk of wasting or gratuitously using big situations." *Letters*, i, 66.

2. *French Poets and Novelists*, p. 82. Compare Swinburne's review of *Les Fleurs du Mal*, in 1862. See Gosse's *Life of Swinburne*, p. 90.

meant by "richness of inspiration" is clear from the essay on Turgénieff, who is described as one of the two foremost living novelists, the other being George Eliot. He is a realist with an "ideal of delicacy." He has all the art of a Flaubert or a Balzac, and something more precious than art which the French novelists do not have, namely, a sound philosophy of life. That is the ultimate test. And a sound philosophy is one that recognizes spiritual values, refinement, purity, abstinence; a good novel is one that illustrates them. It illustrates for example the moral interest of renunciation and suffering as in Turgénieff's *A Nest of Noblemen*. It presents the triumph of soul over sense, thus illustrating the great moral truth that salvation lies in an exercise of the will. James is especially charmed with Turgénieff's heroines, with their purity, strength of will, and power to resist. They remind him of New England women in their virginal "angularity." To Chekhov, who was an admirer of Turgénieff, these saintly heroines seemed Turgénieff's greatest weakness.

The disparagement of Flaubert [1] implied in this contrast cannot be called good criticism. Nothing in Turgénieff illustrates better than *L'Éducation Sentimentale* the principle that salvation is to be found only in an exercise of the will; and the lesson, if it is a lesson one desires, is not the less plain because it is indirect, because there is no greatness or nobility in the book. Time has not sustained James's verdict concerning the relative merit of the two novelists. If morality or richness of inspiration is to be made the final criterion, we should be certain at any rate that it is a sufficiently broad and intelligent morality. It is difficult to escape the impression that James's morality is sometimes only a genteel distaste for the uglier facts of life, and that

1. Compare a view of Flaubert similar to James's in Brunetière's *Histoire et Littérature*, vol. ii, and in his *Le Roman Naturaliste*.

his "richness of inspiration" might upon occasion be more exactly described as *purity* of inspiration, as a kind of conventual fragrance which is the opposite of richness. He talks rather too much about the uncleanness of French literature, and we are forced to remind ourselves that the moralist is not afraid of uncleanness, or of anything except the failure to recognize things for what they are. Morality tends to become identified in James with a "certain charm," and it is a question whether in his strictures on Baudelaire and Flaubert he was too much of a moralist or not enough of one. He might have allowed himself at any rate to be more of a critic.

Though far less conspicuous in the bulk of the essays in *French Poets and Novelists* than in those on Baudelaire and Flaubert, James's hostility to the French point of view is never entirely absent. It leads him to describe *Mlle. de Maupin* as Gautier's one disagreeable performance, and to assert that the preface to that story is deserving of no retort but a laugh. "Poor Gautier," he observes patronizingly, "seems to stand forever in the chill external air which blows over the surface of things." [1] He had the "intelligence of a puppy," and "cared for nothing and knew nothing in men and women but the epidermis." Again Balzac, like Flaubert, lacks "that slight but needful thing — charm." He is neither poet nor moralist but only a great temperament, not like Thackeray, George Eliot, George Sand, a conscience and a mind. That he is sometimes taken seriously in France as a moralist only shows how superficial the French are. His moral obtuseness and lack of taste are best shown in his treatment of women. He cannot depict either a good woman or a fine lady, and his attempts to describe aristocratic manners suggest to James "the dreams of an ambitious hair dresser." A com-

1. Review of Gautier, *North American Review*, October, 1874.

parison of his pictures of provincial life with those of George Eliot, always tolerant and humane, deepens our sense of the meagreness of Balzac's philosophy.[1] As for his beliefs in politics and religion, James sums them up as "pure charlatanism, an elaborate mess of folly."

> But from the moment he ceases to be a simple dramatist, Balzac is an arrant charlatan. It is probable that no equally vigorous mind was ever at pains to concoct such elaborate messes of folly. They spread themselves over page after page, in a close, dense, verbal tissue, which the reader scans in vain for some little flower of available truth.[2]

James is aware that this is not the happiest vein in which to depict the faults of a favorite writer, and he explains that "Balzac himself was brutal and must be handled with his own weapons. It would be absurd to write of him in semi-tones and innuendoes; he never used them himself."[3] It would not have occurred to the young reviewer that any explanation was necessary, nor would it have occurred to the author of *Notes on Novelists* that a want of finesse in his subject could justify an absence of that quality in the critic.

James's admiration for George Sand is haunted by reserves concerning the irregularity of her personal conduct, by her failure to distinguish between virtuous and vicious love, by the fact that she had "morally no taste," as is shown in her treatment of her mother in the memoirs. Her moral vision was imperfect, and her philosophy, viewed "against the light of a certain sort of ripe reason," was exceedingly thin. And of the same nature finally, though less obtrusive than anywhere else in the book, are the critic's reserves concerning de Musset. His "Andalusian

1. Compare Brunetière's similar opinion in his *Le Roman Naturaliste.*
2. *French Poets and Novelists*, p. 112.
3. *Ibid.*

passions" strike James as peculiar in a youth of nineteen; "the pairs of lovers who take refuge from an exhausted vocabulary in biting each other" make the poet's inspiration seem vicious from an Anglo-Saxon point of view.

But these objections are more or less incidental, and the emphasis in the studies just mentioned is upon literary quality rather than upon a writer's intellectual and moral shortcomings as seen by an "Anglo-Saxon mind." A quality and its defects are neatly blended in the following passage:

Infinite are the combinations of our faculties. Some of us are awkward writers and yearning moralists; others are masters of a perfect style which has never reflected a spiritual spark. Gautier's disposition served him to the end, and enabled him to have a literary heritage perfect of its kind. He could look every day at a group of beggars sunning themselves on the Spanish Steps at Rome, against their golden wall of mouldering travertine, and see nothing but the brownness of their rags and their flesh-tints — see it and enjoy it forever, without an hour's disenchantment, without a chance of one of those irresistible revulsions of mood in which the "mellowest" rags are but filth, and filth is poverty, and poverty is a haunting shadow, and picturesque squalor a mockery. His unfaltering robustness of vision — of appetite, one may say — made him not only strong but enviable.[1]

These are Gautier's great qualities, robustness of vision and a perfect style, together with an intellectual passion, which in *Émaux et Camées* makes "an esthetic, an almost technical conviction glow with a kind of moral fervor."

Again, in this passage on Balzac, we are in the critical atmosphere of the essay on Sainte-Beuve.

But behind Balzac's figures we feel a certain heroic pressure that drives them home to our credence — a contagious illusion on the author's own part. The imagination that produced them is

1. *French Poets and Novelists*, p. 70.

working at a greater heat; they seem to proceed from a sort of creative infinite and they help each other to be believed in. It is pictorally a larger, sturdier, more systematic style of portraiture than Turgénieff's. This is altogether the most valuable element in Balzac's novels; it is hard to see how the power of physical evocation can go farther. In future years, if people find his tales, as a whole, too rugged and too charmless, let them take up one occasionally and, turning the leaves, read simply the portraits. In Balzac every one who is introduced is minutely described; if the individual is to say but three words he has the honours of a complete portrait. Portraits shape themselves under his pen as if in obedience to an irresistible force; while the effort with most writers is to collect the material — to secure the model — the effort with Balzac is to disintegrate his visions, to accept only one candidate in the dozen. And it is not only that his figures are so definite, but that they are so plausible, so real, so characteristic, so recognizable. The fertility of his imagination in this respect was something marvellous.[1]

It is the novelist's primary virtue, an "all-devouring love of reality." The *Comédie* has a "thousand faults," but it is a "monumental excuse," and Balzac, like Shakespeare, "may be treated as final authority on human nature."

The essay on Balzac is on the whole the best piece of criticism in the volume, and the strength of James's sympathy and the sureness of his insight are highly significant. He closes the study of George Sand with the statement, "She is an optimist lined with a romancer," and adds, "something even better in a novelist is that tender appreciation of actuality which makes the application of a single coat of rose color seem an act of violence." This springs from a feeling as deep as his disgust with Flaubert's realism. His own vision of experience he regarded as something infinitely finer and deeper than Flaubert's or Balzac's, but in his devotion to it, in the scrupulous art which he

1. *French Poets and Novelists*, p. 124.

lavished upon it, James was in perfect accord with just such a temperament as Flaubert's and could take the full measure of Balzac's great gift. He never felt this radical kinship with Turgénieff, who was too mild and indulgent to have a strong faith in art or in anything else, and this is why the essay on Balzac, despite the critic's numerous cavils, has a warmth altogether lacking in the one on Turgénieff. James could abuse Balzac in the comfortable assurance of a profound sympathy and liking.

Perhaps the happiest example of literary portraiture in *French Poets and Novelists* is the study of de Musset. Here James is in full sympathy with his subject; his imagination glows; his phrases are eloquently right. Like the review of Tennyson's "Queen Mary,"[1] the essay proves that James's sensibility could serve him in poetry as well as in prose, and not as a mere general literary sensibility but in a specifically poetic way. His taste in poetry was limited, to be sure, but in much the same way as his taste in prose. The absence of poetic criticism in his work is only one aspect of a concentration upon contemporary and nearly contemporary prose fiction, which becomes increasingly evident, and probably reflects his actual reading. James was a critic without a library, without a passion for books in the traditional sense. He was moreover too busy to read; his way of life, during his best years, was not the way of the scholar but of the man of the world. The material he sought was the material of fiction, not of criticism. "Reading," he says, "tends to take for me the place of experience." But this was late in life, and the reading, so far as one can tell, was mainly of contemporary fiction. James's experience of books, like his experience of life, had a certain depth and intensity transcending ordinary experience, but it was neither rich nor various.

1. *Views and Reviews.*

But to come back to de Musset. The following passage from the essay indicates the nature of James's taste in poetry:

His verse is not chiselled and pondered, and in spite of an ineffable natural grace, it lacks the positive qualities of cunning workmanship — those qualities which are found in such high perfection in Théophile Gautier. To our own sense Musset's exquisite feeling more than makes up for one half the absence of "chiselling," and the ineffable grace we spoke of just now makes up for the other half. His sweetness of passion, of which the poets who have succeeded him have so little, is a more precious property than their superior science.[1]

The absence of cunning workmanship is, we see, a minor matter compared with de Musset's spontaneity and sweetness of passion, the normality and wholesomeness of his feeling. The contrast with Gautier is the same in principle as the contrast between de Bernard and Flaubert, and here as elsewhere James's preference is for the familiar, the humanly appealing as against innovation and a too serious preoccupation with art.

The essay has charm as well as truth, and a kind of tenderness of insight, the grace of seeing clearly and loving well. The poet is described as "slim and tremulous," deeply and passionately lyrical, "an image of universally sentient youth." Of the closing lines of the "Stanzas to Malibran" James says, "to rise so high, and yet in form, in accent, to remain so still and temperate, belongs only to great poetry." De Musset's plays, in their quality of fancy, their "sentimental perfume" remind the critic of Shakespeare's romantic comedies.

He has, in strictness, only one idea — the idea that the passion of love and the act of loving are the divinest things in a miserable world; that love has a thousand disappointments, deceptions and

1. *French Poets and Novelists*, p. 28.

pangs, but that for its sake they are all worth enduring, and that as Tennyson has said, more curtly, and reservedly,

> 'Tis better to have loved and lost,
> Than never to have loved at all.

. . . . . .

At other times he feels its relation to the other things that make up man's destiny, and the sense of aspiration mingles with the sense of enjoyment or of regret. Then he is at his best; then he seems an image of universally sentient youth.[1]

The most interesting thing in the life of Hawthorne (1879) is its ironic emphasis upon the provincialism of New England. Hawthorne, according to the critic, owes most of his faults to his background; he is thin, meagre, and over-fanciful because the conditions of life in which he found himself were primitive and ugly, devoid of civilizing agencies. It was a great misfortune that he was not born into more humane and congenial surroundings, such as England would have offered. *The American Note-Books* are empty because there was nothing for Hawthorne to observe. He was a "thin New Englander with a miasmatic conscience," and the main fault of *The Scarlet Letter* is its abuse of the fanciful, its want of reality. This is only one side of the picture, and it is by no means so harsh in effect as it appears here, stated briefly and crudely. The exquisite purity and depth of Hawthorne's imagination, the dignity of his themes, the perfection of his style: these and other qualities are deftly traced and unobtrusively related to his defects. The irony is occasionally transparent or forced, the light dismissal of Hawthorne's pessimism as "mere shadowy fancies and conceits" might be questioned. On the other hand, the readableness of the life, its grace of style, is no small thing. For it is after all by virtue of the style that so much of the literary character of Haw-

1. *French Poets and Novelists*, p. 30.

thorne gets itself expressed and lives in James's biography. The note of cosmopolitan worldliness is a little forced; it could scarcely be otherwise, considering in what a near relation James himself stood to Hawthorne's meagre background. He was himself in the very act of escaping, or trying to escape, from the peril which he describes with so much zest and on the whole with so much good humor. Yet no less evident is his sympathy with Hawthorne's New England heritage, with the seafaring ancestors, with all that was clean and straight and manly in Hawthorne's blood. As between the grossness of Balzac, or the moral indifference of Gautier or Flaubert, and the miasmatic conscience of Hawthorne there is no doubt where James's instinctive sympathy lay. For his own part, he would try to combine the worldliness and artistic cunning of the French with a richness of an altogether different kind, the spiritual or moral richness which he felt was the inestimable heritage of the English-speaking community.

CHAPTER THREE

PARTIAL PORTRAITS AND ESSAYS IN LONDON

Just in proportion as he is sentient and restless, just in proportion as he reacts and reciprocates and penetrates, is the critic a valuable instrument; for in literature assuredly criticism *is* the critic, just as art is the artist.   .   .   .   .

James, "Criticism," *Essays in London*

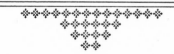

PARTIAL PORTRAITS AND
ESSAYS IN LONDON

THE two volumes which contain the bulk of James's
critical writing from 1883 to 1894, *Partial Portraits*
(1888) and *Essays in London* (1893), define a conception
of criticism very different from the formula of the early
reviews, and more rounded and explicit than the attitude
implied in James's praise of Sainte-Beuve. Not only is the
theory more complete, but it is far more consistently practised. It is expounded in two essays, "The Art of Fiction" [1]
and "Criticism." [2] We hear nothing more of standards;
the artist has supplanted the legislator and judge, and
criticism has become a fine art, the most delicate and personal of fine arts. The stand taken in these essays and
elsewhere in the two volumes is completely evolved, mature and final. It is in accord with James's powers, with
his temperament and his literary preferences. The aston-
ishingly subtle thing about it is that it can go so far in the
direction of appreciation without abandoning these preferences; and it enables James when at his best, as in the
essay on de Maupassant, to do justice both to his own
sense of moral values and to his subject's lack of it. It is
at once a theory of complete artistic freedom and of the
strictest moral accounting. The freedom is a condition of
the accounting; the artist is his own Recording Angel. It
is the critic's care to observe and portray, to put before us
the "revealed identity," the "salient case," without the

1. *Partial Portraits.*   2. *Essays in London.*

presence of which criticism is vain. For criticism is positive, it is "appreciation or it is nothing." "Silence," we
are told, "is the perfection of disapproval." [1]

The critic's passion, like the story-teller's, is "love of
the special case," and both are to be known by their power
of observation and their boundless curiosity. The critic
demands of a subject only that it have an identity, a definable character, and thus in any criticism worth the name
a degree of successful art is taken for granted at the outset.
The beauty of this doctrine — James draws the moral in
emphasizing the superior reticence of French criticism as
compared with English — is that it would still the hubbub
of literary chatter in our periodicals, and so perhaps allow
the voice of criticism to be heard. But how is the case to
be recognized? It is impossible to say, as it is impossible
to tell a writer how to recognize a subject. It is because
he does recognize it, unaided, that he is a writer. And so
with the critic. Lacking taste, the one indispensable thing,
he may have mastered all the standards and formulas in
the world and be helpless. He is as much of an artist in
his own way as the novelist in his, and rules are equally
useless to both. It is the result that explains and justifies
everything, in the novel a "sense of life," in the criticism
a sense of art, which is life clarified and condensed, framed
by a temperament, to which the critic applies himself with
the same free curiosity, the same attention and cunning as
the novelist employs in fixing *his* subject.

To such a critic classes and kinds are no help; the only
useful distinction is between works that are alive and those
that are not.[2] If a novel has life it matters little whether it

1. *Picture and Text*, p. 13.
2. ". . . the only classification of the novel that I can understand,"
writes James, "is into that which has life and that which has it not."
And "to produce the illusion of life" is the beginning and end of the
novelist's whole effort. "The Art of Fiction," *Partial Portraits*, p. 393.

is a novel of manners or adventure, realistic or romantic; the important thing is not how it resembles other novels but how it differs from them. For it is alive precisely by virtue of the difference, by virtue of the particular vision of experience embodied in it. A novel, then, being a "personal impression life," the critic's business is to seize and define that impression, not to obscure it by laboriously fitting the work into some formal and, as likely as not, meaningless category. ". . . there are," says James, "just as many kinds, as many ways, as many forms and degrees of the 'right' as there are personal points of view." [1] The point of view is everything, it is the casket which holds and defines the precious sense of life, and gives form, in the only vital sense of the word, to a work of art.

It is on this account that nothing should be allowed to interfere with the integrity of the artist's vision; it must be free in order to be candid. The complete liberty of the novelist to feel and say, to be true to his perceptions, regardless of public opinion and of all critical rules, distinctions, and classifications, that is the whole burden of "The Art of Fiction." The artist will find his subject wherever the unrestricted play of his temperament leads him to look for it. He must not submit to any external constraint or inner timidity. The province of art is "all life, all observation, all vision"; [2] there is no forbidden ground. A writer may fail because his sensibilities are few or dull, but it may be, as English and American fiction proves, for quite another reason; it may be because, misled by a false convention as to what he *ought* to feel and say, he becomes timid, neglects his sensibilities and ignores his perceptions. What makes a writer like de Maupassant, on the other hand, a "salient case" is the fact that his gifts are strong and that

1. "Mr. Kipling's Early Stories," *Views and Reviews*, p. 228.
2. *Partial Portraits*, p. 399.

he gives them the fullest play, that he "writes directly *from* them."

To quarrel with an artist over his subject is, therefore, the "true stultification of criticism"; it is criticism defeating its own end. According to de Maupassant what the sincere critic says to the writer is simply, "Make me something fine in the form that shall suit you best, according to your temperament." [1] Subjects, ways, and points of view are innumerable; the last thing anyone can do is to dogmatize about them. We are of course at liberty to dislike the idea or the result, in which case we simply let it alone. Taste, James argues, is absolute; there is nothing that one ought to like or to dislike. For the critic moreover the subject does not exist except as the artist has treated it; in the treatment if anywhere lies the clue to a temperament; but the bad critic is only too apt to deceive himself with a pernicious abstraction, to assume the existence of a subject apart from its form and to discuss it as if it were a felt reality in the work itself. Nothing in a novel is subject which is not also treatment; the idea and the form are inseparable, and neither by itself has the slightest reality for the critic.

> Form ist nie ohne Gehalt,
> Gehalt bringt die Form mit.

"We must grant the artist his subject," writes James, "our criticism is applied only to what he makes of it," [2] to the finished product, which is all execution or treatment in the sense that it bears everywhere the stamp of the artist's mind, and both idea and form in so far as the two are inseparable.

Moral criticism is bad in so far as it is criticism of the

1. *Partial Portraits*, p. 245.
2. *Ibid.*, p. 394.

idea apart from its form. How, asks James, can a novel (being a picture) be either moral or immoral? And he adds, ". . . questions of art are questions (in the widest sense) of execution; questions of morality are quite another affair . . ." [1] The moral critic finds that the subject is trivial or unhealthy or one-sided; and at the same time he may have nothing but praise for the writer's style. It is implied thus that no amount of artistic ingenuity can affect the intrinsic badness of certain subjects, and it follows that the artist should avoid these subjects; his freedom is curtailed, more or less according to the standards of his age and country. English fiction has suffered in this way from a "certain diffidence," which is the reverse of moral strength. "If art," writes George Eliot, "does not enlarge men's sympathies, it does nothing morally." [2] True morality as well as true criticism depends upon the artist's freedom to see and describe life in his own way. It is true that the critic is equally free, and may, if he happens to be so constituted, see in a work of art only a nasty "subject." But he is at the same time obliged to be interesting, and if we do not find him so, we simply do not read him.

The beliefs just enumerated were evidently more or less inspired by James's contact with Flaubert and his group. It remained for an American to become one of the missionaries of French Naturalism in England. But the effects of his mission, if it had any, must have been ambiguous, for if he zealously advocated some of the doctrines he no less ardently condemned much of the practice. It is for the literary historian on the other hand to say how much James's own practice contributed to the esthetic mood of the 'nineties in England. It is clear that he was himself but little under the prevailing spell. He regarded the whole

1. *Partial Portraits*, p. 405.
2. Cross, *Life and Letters of George Eliot*, p. 277.

experiment as a failure, for reasons summed up in the following comment upon the earlier esthetic revival.

They [the English] carry on their huge broad back a nameless mountain of conventions and prejudices, a dusky cloud of inaptitudes and fears, which casts a shadow upon the frank and confident practice of art. The consequence of all this is that their revivals of taste are even stranger than the abuses they are meant to correct. They are violent, voluntary, mechanical; wanting in grace, in tact, in the sense of humor and of proportion.[1]

But if the side he presents to the English seems "very artistic" and French, his attitude toward the French themselves is consistently that of the "English-speaking consciousness." He holds to the opinion, as always, that French Naturalism, despite its sincerity and mastery of form, is lacking in those qualities that make art amiable and humanly significant, lacking in vision, in humanity, in a taste for the intangible. And the relation between this attitude and his apparently quite emancipated doctrine is by no means easy to define. He does not quarrel with the artist over his subject, but the subject he tells us nevertheless "matters in the highest degree," for some subjects are "much more remunerative than others," and if we were to "put up a prayer it would be that artists should choose none but the richest."[2] This takes us straight back to the "essential richness of inspiration" doctrine in *French Poets and Novelists*. "There is one point," writes James, "at which the moral sense and the artistic sense lie very near together; that is in the light of the very obvious truth that the deepest quality of a work of art will always be the the quality of the mind of the producer," for it is an axiom that "no good novel will ever proceed from a super-

1. *Partial Portraits*, p. 371. Compare the essay on D'Annunzio in *Notes on Novelists*.
2. *Partial Portraits*, p. 396.

ficial mind," an axiom that "will cover all needful moral ground." [1] A novel it is true is neither moral nor immoral, but its excellence depends upon the intensity and fullness of the individual impression of life recorded in it, and so ultimately upon the fineness and depth of the writer's vision. It is not a work of art at all unless it is in some degree, however small, illustrative. But it is a great work only when it is largely illustrative, when it has an abundance of meaning. And what produces this abundance is "the enveloping air of the artist's humanity—a widely and wondrously varying element; being on one occasion a rich and magnificent medium, and on another a comparatively poor and ungenerous one." [2] The critic's judgment, being in the last analysis an estimate of the artist's quality of mind, is at once moral and esthetic. [3]

This is the essence of James's morality, and it springs from his guiding conviction that a book is first and last the expression of a temperament. A perception of things which is habitually low or narrow is as fatal to art as it is to conduct.

But if that is so we find a curious exception in de Maupassant, who was undeniably a master, and yet, as the critic points out, little better than a clever animal, brutal, cynical, and indifferent to all that is delicate and noble. How did he manage to be an artist, perhaps a great artist? He is a "lion in the path of the moralist"; but there is a way, so James reasons, of circumventing him. The way, it appears, is to recognize that de Maupassant is strong, not as one might suppose, in spite of his limited vision but largely because of it. It is just because he omits one of the

1. *Partial Portraits*, p. 406.
2. *Novels and Tales*, vol. iii, Preface, p. x.
3. Compare Milton's "I was confirmed in this opinion, that he who would not be frustrated of his hope to write well hereafter in laudable things ought himself to be a true poem."

"items in the problem," all that part of human nature which has to do with conduct and "operative character," that perfection is comparatively easy for him. He rejects analysis and confines himself to the objective, the "epic" manner, not from choice as he would have us believe, but because he lacks the vision for analysis, for "psychology." All he knows is what his senses tell him, though in this knowledge he is to the last degree a master. It is discouraging to find what "low views" are compatible with being a master, but the moralist, recognizing the true source of de Maupassant's mastery, reflects that he has his perfection upon terms so ugly as to make it not worth having to a writer of "Anglo-Saxon faith," and reflects also that the finer vision at the service of a talent equal to de Maupassant's will produce another and immeasurably higher perfection. This, it may be noted in passing, was part of James's ambition as a story-teller, the high romantic aim, the "figure in the carpet." It was to be thoroughly English in perception and feeling, wholly French in execution; to make the history of a "fine conscience" as palpable as the history of Emma Bovary, as firmly wrought and inescapably "told."

The reasoning with reference to de Maupassant is a little difficult to follow. If it is true in the first place that questions of art are only questions of execution in the widest sense, and questions of morality an altogether different affair, why is the critic at such pains to condemn de Maupassant's particular angle of vision, to formulate a moral judgment about it? Or is execution to be understood in a sense so wide as to include subject? Further, by James's logic de Maupassant is not merely an exception to the rule which makes artistic value dependent upon the artist's general humanity; he is a direct contradiction of it, illustrating an opposite rule, to the effect roughly, that perfection in art may depend upon meagreness of insight. One may differ and draw the inference instead that James's moral criteria have little to do with a writer's success or failure, and that the "enveloping air of the artist's humanity" is a negligible or at best a very uncertain criterion of art. James's whole point lies of course in the distinction between a lower art, perfect of its kind, and a higher. There are people who refuse to see any meaning in such a distinction, and at times James himself seems to be one of them, as for example, when he asserts that "no work of art is absolutely little." [1] But in this essay James is avowedly both critic and moralist, and it is in the latter capacity that he applies to de Maupassant the test of an English sensibility, which includes faith in character, in the power to renounce, to suffer, and to live in the spirit, as well as kindness and humor. It may be argued that it would have been enough to show how de Maupassant differs in sensibility from George Eliot, let us say, without making the difference a text for a sermon, or implying that the former would have been a greater artist had he possessed the conscience of the latter. But though the critic's characteristically supple effort to do justice to both the moral and artistic aspects of his subject is not free from ambiguity, it is the ambiguity not of a vague or confused but of a subtle and complex point of view.

The essential thing after all is the vividness of portrayal in the essay. For the shadow of James's disapproval does not darken the subject, as in much of his earlier criticism, but sets it off rather, heightening certain traits, and by the same stroke fixing the critic's angle of vision, his "special window." In the earlier criticism there is frequently nothing but shadow or at the best a somewhat awkward balancing of praise and blame. Here everything is related in the

1. *Picture and Text*, p. 77.

effort to portray an identity, subtly and persistently related, and next to the vividness of the result nothing is more evident than the condition imposed by the nature of the critic's prepossessions. His morality is his particular way of seeing, and the point is that he sees a great deal, perhaps neither because of his morality nor in spite of it, but because he has excellent vision.

His ideal in criticism is exactly the same as his ideal in fiction and in the conduct of life. It is to be "indefatigably supple." The most prominent characters in his later novels are critics of life in just this sense, people of inordinate, or extravagant sensibility, precisely like their creator in all but the habit of writing books. The capacity for feeling life, measured by the number and intensity of one's impressions, that is the sum of all virtue in conduct as in art. There is no vice but coarseness. In criticism "the only kind worth speaking of is the kind that springs from the liveliest experience." Upon the critic falls a double responsibility, "for he deals with life at second-hand as well as at first." [1]

To lend himself, to project himself and steep himself, to feel and feel till he understands, and to understand so well that he can say, to have perception at the pitch of passion and expression as embracing as the air, to be infinitely curious and incorrigibly patient, and yet plastic and inflammable and determinable, stooping to conquer and serving to direct — these are fine chances for an active mind, chances to add the idea of independent beauty to the conception of success. Just in proportion as he is sentient and restless, just in proportion as he reacts and reciprocates and penetrates, is the critic a valuable instrument . . .[2]

"Perception at the pitch of passion and expression as embracing as the air," this together with the novelist's love of the "special case" is the principle of James's best criti-

1. *Essays in London*, p. 265.   2. *Ibid.*, p. 264.

cism. Its tools are the "kindly, disinterested palette and brush," its object "to fix a face and figure . . . to catch a talent in the fact, follow its line, and put a finger on its essence." [1] It is never bald or general, though it may be highly illustrative, like the portrait of a character in a story. The meaning it strives for is some truth about art, some law of the creative mind, a meaning inherent always in the concrete example, the problem or "case," which is instructive and welcome to the critic in proportion as it is a "challenge to interpretation." The critic's morality is so qualified and assimilated, so fully related to the perception of literary values, as to bear in effect little resemblance to the downright morality of the earlier criticism, though it is in substance the same. The art of criticism becomes in James's hands more and more an art of insinuating reserves, of subtly and delicately enmeshing the subject in a multitude of fine perceptions. Whatever else it may be James's perception is never coarse. It feels its way at once ardently and delicately, always to the remotest implications of things, to the finer shades of truth. If it hovers too long over minor niceties and loses in the effort a certain robustness and breadth of vision, the loss is at once deliberate and characteristic. Truth is only fineness of truth, and it is the single aim of critic and novelist alike. Fineness implies a jealous economy, the unravelling of an impression down to its last and minutest thread. No shade or implication but is worth saving, and fineness of truth is equivalent to the whole truth, and is equivalent moreover not as an accumulation of particles but as a totality, as a group of relationships, not accidental but necessary. Thus it is that we begin to feel in the essay on the de Goncourts a new closeness of texture, a kind of breathless circling about the object, which is brought to perfection only in *Notes on*

1. *Partial Portraits*, pp. 137, 138.

Novelists. But there is already a perceptible difference in style between *Partial Portraits* and *Essays in London*, the earlier and later volumes. The sentences in the *Essays* are longer, more involved, more intricately qualified, the effort of the style is to embrace rather than to point to, and as far as possible to embrace the whole object at once.

As in the essay on de Maupassant, so in the treatment of other writers more or less in the Flaubert tradition, James's criticism is haunted by a never-failing sense of the contrast between English soundness of feeling and French superficiality. But the obtrusiveness of the feeling varies; it is far less noticeable in the study of Daudet,[1] for example, than elsewhere. James had a personal fondness for his subject; and besides, Daudet was not ridden by "realistic" doctrines, he was romantic, he had gaiety, humor, and poetry;[2] and he was likable as a man. Yet for all its fine appreciativeness, its tact, good feeling and happiness of phrase, the essay ends upon the familiar note, want of moral insight, of "high imagination," and "consequently of ideas." It is a "partial portrait" in the sense that James, as he intimates, is more indulgent than he should be towards Daudet's failings. It must be remembered that James was exceedingly sensitive to personal impressions, and that he had known many of the writers whom he discusses. His criticism is sometimes reminiscent and personal rather than critical, portraiture of the man rather than the writer, ostensibly so in the commemorative essay on Turgénieff, and less obviously in the essays on Stevenson and Lowell, where distinctness of judgment is blurred by a friendly mist, or in that of Flaubert, where one may feel

1. *Partial Portraits.* Compare an essay on Daudet of the preceding year in the *Atlantic Monthly* for June, 1882.

2. Compare the similar view of Brunetière in the essay "L'Impressionisme" (1879) in *Le Roman Naturaliste.*

that a personal dislike for the subject lurks somewhere behind a suavely patronizing and much qualified belittlement. It is the theory of portraying a temperament, carried to an extreme; it is always, whether favorable or otherwise, an estimate of the artist's "humanity," a moral judgment, peculiarly applicable to some of the French Naturalists, whose art seemed to James, from any other point of view, so flawless, and applicable also to some of James's English subjects, who were deficient in art but admirable in feeling.

The application is not free from the complacency of a superior moral tone, and the treatment of Loti, the de Goncourts, and Flaubert is accompanied more or less distinctly by the refrain, Thank God we are not as the French are. It emphasizes proudly the "natural decorum of the English spirit," its good form, reticence, and respectability as much as its moral soundness. To James's mind these qualities indeed constituted its moral soundness in a considerable measure; a nasty or indiscreet word was almost, if not quite, as reprehensible as an ugly deed. Here as in *French Poets and Novelists* his morality strikes one as lacking in seriousness and candor, as being too gravely concerned about appearances, as emanating from a polite English drawing-room and having about it the taint of Pharisaism. In his own fiction his care was not to eschew adultery but to keep it out of sight, to keep it above all from seeming gross. His attitude toward French fiction seems less weighty and straightforward than the attitude of a moralist like Brunetière. It was an attitude already out of touch with the most advanced taste in England when James wrote, and perhaps more in accord with the literary partialities of Boston than with those of London. The critic is frankly complacent about the superior morality of the English. He alludes, for example, to Loti's exoticism,[1] his brilliant success in "changing his skin," and observes that Loti's preference is usually for a "dusky one." Rarely, says the critic, does he attempt to assume the "complexion of one of the fairer races — of the English, for instance, the fairest perhaps of all." Again, English gallantry would forbid so brutal an exposure of feminine weakness as the de Goncourts' *Journal* flaunts before the face of the public. Like Brunetière James makes much of George Eliot's superiority to the French realists, which is due to her profound sympathy with her kind and the total absence of the vice, characteristic of French writers from Balzac down, of an unrelenting, narrow, and unintelligible hatred of the *bourgeoisie*, which makes their art invidious and unamiable.

Loti's art is exquisite,[2] so fine that we are apt to overlook his "commonness," his "vulgarity of spirit and thinness of inspiration," which is the penalty of ignoring "the phenomena of character and the higher kinds of sensibility." It is a penalty to which the French are all subject. "As painters they go straight to the mark, as analysts they only scratch the surface." Characters without moral feeling and a sense of responsibility cannot be made interesting. Thus Loti, when he talks of love, seems not to be talking of affection, a habit which is characteristically French, and to James's mind very odd. There is indeed some moral feeling in *Mon Frère Yves* and in *Pêcheur d'Islande*, but in the latter it is after all the "senses that vibrate most," and the characters in it are infinitely less "complicated" than most of the characters in "valid works of fiction." But for all this there is no denying the greatness of Loti's art; and not until the golden age comes, the happy eventuality touched upon in the study of de Maupassant, when writers — they will not be French —"for whom the life of

1. *Essays in London*, p. 176.   2. *Ibid.*, p. 158.

the soul is real" have learned to write, not until then will the art of such as Loti encounter really formidable competition.

If they have almost nothing to show us in the way of the operation of character, the possibilities of conduct, the part played in the world by the *idea* (you would never guess, either from Pierre Loti or from M. Guy de Maupassant, that the idea has any force or any credit in the world); if man, for them, is the simple sport of fate, with suffering for his main sign — either suffering or one particular satisfaction, always the same — their affirmation of all this is still, on the whole, the most complete affirmation that the novel at present offers us. They have on their side the accident, if accident it be, that they never cease to be artists. They will keep this advantage till the optimists of the hour, the writers for whom the life of the soul is equally real and visible (lends itself to effects and triumphs, challenges the power to "render") begin to seem to them formidable competitors.[1]

"Art," says James with reference to the de Goncourts' *Journal*, "is most in character when it most shows itself amiable." [2] That is the theme of his criticism of the *Journal* as of Flaubert's letters. It is criticism of the man and turns as usual upon the seeming paradox that great artistic gifts do not always imply a corresponding greatness of temper. They seem compatible on the contrary not only with an absence of ideas and moral feeling as in de Maupassant, Daudet, and Loti, but as shown by the de Goncourts and Flaubert with a complete want of serenity and generosity of spirit as well, with meanness, irritability, and vindictiveness. "It is always a pain to perceive that some of the qualities we prize don't imply the others." The "confusion between esthetics and ill-humor" fostered by the example of the de Goncourts is regrettable. Admirable as they are in certain respects as writers, or better as painters, for their whole virtue lies in their pictorial

1. *Essays in London*, p. 183.   2. *Ibid.*, p. 193.

power, they are contemptible as men. The "natural decorum of the English spirit" recoils from their systematic
treachery and malice towards their contemporaries, illustrated in their malevolent pursuit of Sainte-Beuve, from
their treatment of women, their obscenity and irritability.
They have not only betrayed their contemporaries, but
they have most flagrantly of all betrayed themselves. They
should have burned their *Journal*, remarks James, if they
wished their novels to be admired, or destroyed the novels
if they wished the *Journal* to be forgotten. Their self-
betrayal is comparable to the indiscreet exposure of Flaubert's epileptic fits. Where will modern literary indiscre-
tion end? And what could have been the manners of good
society in France if the picture in the *Journal* is true?
English life at any rate offers no parallel to such a picture.
The de Goncourts imply that for "people of masculine
observation the term delicacy has no relevancy at all."
As to which James's characteristic comment is that delicacy represents a state of perception, and that without it
one is in danger of feeling coarsely, of being in other words
esthetically as well as morally obtuse. And this coarsening
of perception comes about from a too prolonged study of
trivial, ugly, and unclean things. For example, the *Journal*
reports a conversation in which Gautier describes the kind
of shoes ballet dancers wear, and how the dancers prepare
the shoes with their own hands. The description is empha-
sized as something of great interest. To James it seems
merely a trivial fact without significance, and the importance attached to it by the de Goncourts a sign of their
want of seriousness. Almost the only friendly picture in
the Journal is that of Gautier, and the friendliness of it is
a sad reflection upon the de Goncourts' taste, while the
portrait itself is, without intending to be, a worse betrayal
than any of the others.

Again in the article on Flaubert's letters [1] the short-comings of the man tend to overshadow the greatness of the writer, and even this greatness is doubtful. The author of *Madame Bovary* is delicately rolled up and well-nigh forgotten in a spidery net-work of destructive analysis. It is an apology for Flaubert and a masterpiece in the art of faint praise. It is pitying, reluctant, and elegiac. The key-note is "poor Flaubert," tortured and unhappy in his personal life, only a splendid failure after all in his art, which with the possible exception of *Madame Bovary* is only "infinitely curious," an "affair of pure esthetics" and "cold as death." James's opinion had not altered in the least since the summary judgment of Flaubert, some twenty years before, in *French Poets and Novelists*. To fellow-craftsmen he is an "inspiring image," but not so much for what he achieved as for the way he strove. Yet few can take his great question seriously, and his devotion to it is a little absurd, like "a life laid down for grammar." James's tone, everything considered a very curious one, is that of the well-bred man of the world to whom an absorb-ing preoccupation of any kind must seem a little ridiculous; it is a tone of patronage concerning the meagreness of Flau-bert's personal life and the ascetic unworldly devotion to an ideal goal. Or it might be described as the broad, good-humored, slightly matter-of-fact English wonder at fanati-cism or any extremity of logic, a state of mind which shades off into Philistinism. The letters, like the de Goncourts' Journal, should never have been published; they "hand him [Flaubert] over to the Philistines with every weakness exposed, every mystery dispelled, every secret betrayed." He shares the narrowness of spirit, the superficiality of his colleagues, their "puerile" hatred of the *bourgeoisie*, which in him amounts to a hatred of all life. He "took life as

1. *Essays in London.*

73

men take a violent toothache." "What," asks James, "has become of ultimate good-humor and the enduring *man*?" Why did Flaubert not make of art itself a refuge — as James was doing? The reason is that he did not after all have sufficient faith even in art, that he remained content with the surface of life, that he "hovered forever at the public door." He should have gone further into the temple; "he should at least have listened to the chamber of the soul." His failure as a man is thus intimately related to his failure as an artist, like the failure of de Maupassant and the de Goncourts.

Why feel, and feel genuinely, so much about "art," in order to feel so little about its privilege? Why proclaim it on the one hand the holy of holies, only to let your behavior confess it on the other a temple open to the winds? Why be angry that so few people care for the real thing, since this aversion of the many leaves a luxury of space? The answer to these too numerous questions is the final perception that the subject of our observations failed of happiness, failed of temperance, not through his excesses, but absolutely through his barriers. He passed his life in strange oblivion of the circumstance that, however incumbent it may be on most of us to do our duty, there is, in spite of a thousand narrow dogmatisms, nothing in the world that any one is under the least obligation to *like* — not even (one braces one's self to risk the declaration) a particular kind of writing. Particular kinds of writing may sometimes, for their producers, have the good fortune to please; but these things are windfalls, pure luxuries, not resident even in the cleverest of us as natural rights. Let Flaubert always be cited as one of the devotees and even, when people are fond of the word, as one of the martyrs of the plastic idea; but let him be still more considerately preserved and more fully presented as one of the most conspicuous of the faithless.[1]

The essay, despite its seemingly "partial" tone, perhaps because of it, is the least sympathetic of all and the least illuminating. The "case" against Flaubert is much the

1. *Essays in London*, p. 149.

same as in contemporary French criticism, like that of Faguet, but the effect of it in James's subtle hands is far more comprehensive and damaging. The antipathy has been ascribed to a personal affront. It might have been expected that James of all men would sympathize with Flaubert's great question; but the latter's consecration seemed to him at once notable and barren, an example of singular devotion which somehow failed to be honorable. Granting that Flaubert's career is in this sense an anomaly James could not have explained it otherwise than by imputation of Flaubert's art. Here as in the example of the de Goncourts and de Maupassant the honor of the craft is at stake, and most of all in Flaubert, since he is generally taken to be the very type of the artist and craftsman.

James's native predilection for the "quiet English heart" appears in his treatment of Trollope, George Eliot, Lowell, and Browning. The essay on Trollope [1] is luminous and genial. It makes much of that writer's natural kindness, of his "tender and friendly feeling about human perplexities," his robust and manly good sense. As contrasted with the "concentrated, sedentary" school of French Naturalists, he was a novelist "who hunted the fox." He is the embodiment of the English "amateur" spirit, yet in his easygoing way he tells us more about life than the French Naturalists, his genius has a freer range, he is more at home in the moral world. His vision is not "that narrow vision of humanity which accompanies the strenuous work offered us in such abundance by the votaries of art for art who sit so long at their desks in Parisian *quatrièmes*." Trollope more than atones for his want of doctrine and his occasional artistic frivolity by his delicacy of feeling, his sympathetic interest in character, his good humor and good sense.

1. *Partial Portraits.*

75

The moral and social interest which gives Trollope his advantage over the French is even greater of course in George Eliot.[1] It is too great, too deliberate, and her work suffers from an "absence of free esthetic life," from "meditation which mitigates the sharpness of portraiture." She did not see in the "irresponsible, plastic way." This was owing, James thinks, to the influence of Lewes as well as to the irregularity of George Eliot's union with him, which prompted a kind of "compensatory earnestness" in her. Yet the greatness of her imagination was after all equal to the depth and seriousness of her mind, and if she had "all the advantages of knowledge," she enjoyed no less "all the luxuries of feeling." At its best her work is completely alive, and it is always spacious and noble, with a "fragrance of moral elevation" about it, and the light of a serene and vigorous mind. Her moral and philosophic preoccupations "raised the roof and widened the area of her esthetic structure," which was yet for the most part if not always founded upon observed realities. James's manner in the two studies devoted to George Eliot is extremely happy, and the "Conversation on Daniel Deronda"[2] (1876) is a perfect example of the critical dialogue, having all the ease of talk and all the precision of good writing, in which the opposing views, representing both extremes and a conciliatory middle ground, are firmly though lightly and humorously discriminated, and the whole discussion has movement, direction, and point.

The essay on Lowell[3] disclaims both the detachment of criticism and the completeness of a portrait. Its tone is that of eulogy and friendly reminiscence, of admiration and pride, perfect in taste and feeling, yet by no means uncritical. It has, like most of the essays in the volume, the effect of composition, of a unifying tone which harmonizes

1. *Partial Portraits.*   2. *Ibid.*   3. *Essays in London.*

a variety of detail, qualifying all without obscuring anything, and giving the essay as a whole an extraordinary closeness of texture. The effect becomes more pronounced in *Notes on Novelists*, and in this respect alone James's criticism is a fine art. What seems to touch the critic's imagination most about Lowell is his success with the English. The community of language and traditions between England and America is, as usual, uppermost in James's mind, and Lowell appeals to him as the symbol of that bond, and of the particular channel in which its force is greatest and its action most direct — the literary. Lowell is a good American in the best English sense. Unlike Hawthorne and Emerson he is not in the least provincial,[1] his love of life is more robust than theirs, his knowledge of the world greater, yet he is never for a moment anything but a good New Englander. And above all else there are his basic English qualities, his sane morality, optimism, and positive temper, the masculine promptings of the "quiet English heart."

He was strong without narrowness, he was wise without bitterness and glad without fatuity. That appears for the most part the temper of those who speak from the quiet English heart, the steady pulses of which were the sufficient rhythm of his eloquence.[2]

Again the tone of an occasion — memorable to some who were present — is finely sustained without any loss of discrimination in the commemorative address, "Browning in Westminster Abbey." It is compact and brilliantly phrased, yet fully rounded and unhurried. It is at once gravely responsible, eloquent, and revealing. And it is above all deeply and reverently English.

1. But compare James's article on Lowell in the *Library of the World's Best Literature*, vol. xvi. "The old Puritan conscience was deep in him, with its strong and simple vision, even in esthetic things, of evil and of good . . ."

2. *Essays in London*, p. 80.

For the great value of Browning is that at bottom, in all the deeply spiritual and human essentials, he is unmistakably in the great tradition — is, with all his Italianisms and cosmopolitanisms . . . a magnificent example of the best and least dilettantish English spirit.

.   .   .   .

He was, indeed, a wonderful mixture of the universal and the alembicated. But he played with the curious and the special, they never submerged him, and it was a sign of his robustness that he could play to the end. His voice sounds loudest, and also clearest, for the things that, as a race, we like best — the fascination of faith, the acceptance of life, the respect for its mysteries, the endurance of its charges, the vitality of the will, the validity of character, the beauty of action, the seriousness, above all, of the great human passion.[1]

At its best the work of this period represents in certain respects the height of James's achievement. If it is less original, less perfect in form, and less searching about matters of art than the prefaces and *Notes on Novelists*, it is also stronger, more vivid, and readable, perhaps on the whole more successful as literary portraiture. Nothing could be better in this kind than the essays on de Maupassant and Trollope, the former of which illustrates so well that fusion of a hostile point of view with a commanding insight which *French Poets and Novelists* fails to achieve. And even where in *Essays in London* James's hostility to the French Naturalists is most conspicuous, his sense for quality, for the graces of form and style, and his power of fixing the very essence of the thing are almost never at fault. His picture of New England provincialism in the Emerson essay [2] is gentler, and more urbane, more deftly related to the subject as well as more penetrating than his treatment of the theme in the life of Hawthorne. Again, for intelligence about art, it would be difficult to match

1. *Essays in London*, p. 228.   2. *Partial Portraits.*

"The Art of Fiction" by any other short essay on the subject, in English at least.

In its power of characterization, of evoking the peculiar vision of things which lives in a successful work of art, of reflecting a writer's mind and soul by a deft and busy accumulation of detail lies the value of the best work in these volumes. It depends upon a delicate perception of literary quality and upon refinement and vividness of style; it is criticism in which sensibility, imagination, a feeling for shades, differences, and implications, and a literary gift of a high order are indispensable. Its relation to the work of Sainte-Beuve is obvious, and there is little doubt that up to this time at least James was a conscious disciple. His sense for character explains many of his qualities as a critic: his preference for people he had actually known or seen, his indifference to literary history, to types and masterpieces and general ideas, his taste for problems, "cases," ironic contradictions. And as he probes deeper in his latest criticism he is always busy with something odd, elusive — the irony in an artistic temperament and career. It is an interest which differs little in a way from what engages him for the most part in his latest fiction. If historically and otherwise his range is narrow as compared with that of Sainte-Beuve or of lesser critics — it becomes later in another sense very wide indeed, embracing nothing less than the motives and meaning of art itself.

CHAPTER FOUR

PREFACES AND NOTES
ON NOVELISTS

At any rate he [Björnson] sounds in your picture — to say nothing of looking in his own! — like the sort of literary fountain from which I am ever least eager to drink; the big, splashing, blundering genius of the hit-or-miss, the *à peu près*, family — without perfection, or the effort toward it, without the exquisite, the love of selection: a big superabundant and promiscuous democrat.

James, *Letters*, i, 221

It is art that *makes* life, makes interest, makes importance, for our consideration and application of these things, and I know of no substitute whatever for the force and beauty of its process. . . . . . .

James, *Letters*, ii, 490

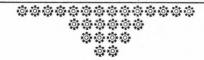

PREFACES AND NOTES
ON NOVELISTS

A DEFINITIVE edition [1] of James's novels and tales was decided upon during his visit to America in 1905. The work of selection and revision, and the writing of prefaces was begun in the following year and completed in 1908. These prefaces are sixteen in number. James found them, he says, "difficult to do, but of a jolly interest." "They are, in general," he writes to Howells, "a sort of plea for Criticism, for Discrimination, for Appreciation on other than infantile lines. . . . They ought, collected together . . . to form a sort of comprehensive manual or *vade-mecum* for aspirants in our arduous profession." [2] As a craftsman — and there was never a more cunning or deliberate one — he understood the reason of and had a theory for everything he did. The prefaces are the best possible commentaries on his own work; they are the fruit of a long career, characterized by a single-minded devotion to the art of letters. "There is the story of one's hero," James writes in the preface to *The Ambassadors*, "and then, thanks to the intimate connexion of things, the story of of one's story itself." [3] In spite of the absence of any trace of pedantry in James's reflections, and their exquisitely urbane and confidential manner, "the story of one's story" is much more than artless gossip or fond reminiscence. The

1. *Novels and Tales*, New York, 1907. All following references are to this edition.
2. *Letters*, ii, 99.   3. *The Ambassadors*, Preface, p. x.

prefaces are deeply luminous, and their light is projected mainly upon two things: James's general theory with respect to fiction and the whole province of art, and the special technique illustrated in his stories.

It is impossible not to dwell for a moment on the literary charm of these after-thoughts. One is reminded of a phrase from James's brilliant little story, "The Death of the Lion," "the overflow into talk of an artist's amorous plan." They glow with the ardor of a creative imagination, deeply and richly conscious of the laws of its operation, recovering easily and everywhere the guiding impulse of its past performance, delighting in difficulties met, in triumphs achieved by scrupulous adherence to a fine artistic faith, the faith that design and lucidity and meaning are everything and that beauty is their authentic symbol. It amounts to a passion, to a restrained and finely tempered one, tempered by an extraordinarily close and exacting play of mind, as also by the ultimate grace of a discreet irony. And the explication, the hard critical nuggets, are enveloped in a tender and romantic atmosphere of reminiscence. James's sense for the past, for the romance and poetry of vanished things, recurs with a soft persistence throughout the prefaces. He is speaking of the Washington he knew before the Civil War. "So, quite exquisitely, as whenever that lapse occurs, the lost presence, the obliterated scene, translated itself for me at last into terms of almost more than earthly beauty and poetry . . . the other, the superseded Washington of the exquisite springtime, of the earlier initiation, of the hovering plaintive ghosts, reduced itself to a great vague blur of warmth and color and fragrance." [1] He is acutely susceptible to the magic of atmosphere in the great European cities, Paris, London, Rome, Florence, where so many of his stories were con-

1. *Lady Barbarina*, Preface, pp. xxi, xxii.

ceived and written. Of the composition of *The American*
in Paris, he writes, "I saw from one day to another my
particular cluster of circumstances, with the life of the
splendid city playing up in it like a flashing fountain in
a marble basin." [1] And again, "through casements open
to the last mildness of the year, a belated Saint Martin's
summer, the tale was taken up afresh by the charming
light click and clatter, that sound as of the thin, quick,
quite feminine surface-breathing of Paris, the shortest of
rhythms for so huge an organism." [2] Of *The Portrait of a
Lady* he writes, "There are pages of the book which in
reading over have seemed to make me see again the brist-
ling curve of the wide Riva [the Riva degli Schiavoni in
Venice], the large colour-spots of the balconied houses and
the repeated undulation of the little hunch-backed bridges,
marked by the rise and drop again, with the wave, of
foreshortened, clicking pedestrians." [3]

In the early Conversation on "Daniel Deronda," written
during James's residence in Paris, the principal speaker
observes that "there is little art in *Deronda*," but a "vast
amount of life," and adds, "In life without art you can
find your account, but art without life is a poor affair." [4]
It is a very different interpretation of the word which
leads James many years later to assert that "art *makes*
life." [5] For in the first place, "it prolongs, it preserves, it
consecrates." [6] Life is only a "splendid waste" or a dull
chaos; it is helpless without the process which gives it
form and beauty, and beauty is expression and "expression is creation and makes the reality." This was Flaubert's belief, to which James inclines, and further that "in
literature we move through a blest world in which we know

1. *The American*, Preface, p. viii. 2. *Ibid.*, p. xii.
3. *The Portrait of a Lady*, Preface, p. vi. 4. *Partial Portraits*, p. 92.
5. *Letters*, ii, 490. 6. *Picture and Text*, p. 134.

nothing except by style, but in which also everything is saved by it, and in which the image is thus always superior to the thing itself." [1] The supreme faculty of the artist is his sense of life, the fine tact which enables him to recognize and to invoke at will the characteristic note, to discriminate what is vital and of the essence of the thing from the accidental and the trivial, for art is no mere transcript, no mere transfer or copy of some real happening; it is a chemical process by which life is prepared for a new function, transformed and improved so as to give it a meaning and make it illustrative.[2] That it takes a great deal of life, of civilized life, and much genius and beauty to produce a little literature, and that the product is worth what it costs, is an idea to which James recurs often.[3] Art, moreover, is an escape; "it muffles the ache of the actual"; [4] it is an escape from the common, the prosaic, the immediate. The artist himself finds an occasional escape from life in his "incurable disposition to interest himself less in his own (always so quickly stale) experience . . . than in that of conceivable fellow-mortals." [5] His life is all perception and imagination; all his achievement is but the rescue of meaning, yet in his contemplative wonder he may enjoy a far richer life than falls to the lot of his simpler fellows. "To criticize," writes James, "is to appropriate, to take intellectual possession." Such a life may be "actively, luxuriously lived," the luxury consisting in the number of its "moral vibrations, well-nigh unrestricted." [6]

1. *Notes on Novelists*, p. 100.
2. *Ibid.*, p. 275.
3. See *French Poets and Novelists*, p. 38; Hawthorne, p. 3; *Notes on Novelists*, p. 191.
4. *Ibid.*, p. 436; *Picture and Text*, p. 150.
5. *Lady Barbarina*, Preface, p. xx.
6. *In the Cage*, Preface, p. xx.

For James art was method, and the problems of method, he tells us, "are the noblest speculations that can engage the human mind." [1] Nothing can exceed his sense for the "refinements and ecstasies of method." [2] "A plan of absolutely definite and measurable application . . . that in itself is always a mark of beauty." [3] He does not see how "a coherent picture of anything is producible save by a complex of fine measurements." [4] Such pictures are not common, the taste for them is rare, and the artist who believes that "composition alone is positive beauty" soon realizes that his conviction must be "sweated for and paid for." [5] Nevertheless beauty in a work of art is always "the close, the curious, the deep." [6] It is the fruit of a process, of a manipulation more or less subtle, the one object of which is to express fully, entirely, "to pump the case gaspingly dry," [7] to squeeze out value to the last drop. And it should be remembered that value for James resided almost wholly in the delicate vibrations of an intensely conscious inward life. He deplores the "hopeless, bemuddled waste" due to an absence of art in Tolstoy, the failure of form in Dostoieffsky,[8] in Balzac; a "conscious negation of method" [9] as the one flaw in Stevenson's intelligence, and admires on the other hand the "beauty of intention and effect"[10] in Flaubert, whose mastery of form, a thing almost unknown in English fiction, enables him in *Bovary* to triumph even over the question of value and to make

1. *Letters*, i, 324.
2. *The Ambassadors*, Preface, p. xxii.
3. *What Maisie Knew*, Preface, p. x.
4. *The American*, Preface, p. xv.
5. *The Ambassadors*, Preface, p. xvii.
6. *The Aspern Papers*, Preface, p. xxi.
7. *The Awkward Age*, Preface, p. xxiii.
8. *Letters*, ii, 237, 324.
9. *Notes on Novelists*, p. 15.
10. *Ibid.*, pp. 90, 91.

things "big" which are intrinsically small. Method includes style, and it is above all the power of style that makes *Bovary* "big." For "there is no complete creation without style any more than there is complete music without sound." [1] One finds this lesson of style in D'Annunzio, where the fusion of substance and form is complete, as in Flaubert, and the "fact of artistic creation is registered at a stroke," so that D'Annunzio's lovely appearances and distinction of form, like Flaubert's, conceal the inherent poverty of his material. He has, says James, "the supremely interesting quality in the novelist that he *fixes* as it were the tone of every cluster of objects he approaches, fixes it by the intensity and consistency of his reproduction." [2] It is style again that saves George Sand, it is the one thing by which her work will live, and it has given to the records of her personal life, in many ways so ugly and trivial, the effect and "achieved dignity" of something tragic. The most hopeful of his young contemporaries was, in James's opinion, Compton Mackenzie, and the most promising thing about him next to his regard for composition and design in the larger sense was his care for style. Yet the efficacy of form has its limits, it will not save a vulgar or barren subject, and the success of D'Annunzio and even to a certain extent of Flaubert is only partial — as we shall see later.

We sometimes talk as if the artist's or novelist's direct experience, the range of his observation of life, were a thing separate from the activity of his imagination. Yet they are really inseparable. A more fruitful distinction would be between the imaginatively unabsorbed, face-value experience of the ordinary person, and the subtle mixture of the observed and the imagined, assimilated under a glow of perception, which constitutes the experience of the

1. *Notes on Novelists*, p. 255.   2. *Ibid.*, p. 274.

novelist. "If one was to undertake to tell tales," writes James, "it could be but because 'notes' had been from the cradle the ineluctable consequence of one's greatest inward energy: to take them was as natural as to look, to think, to feel, to recognize, to remember, to perform any act of understanding." [1] Experience is "the very atmosphere of the mind; and when the mind is imaginative ... it takes to itself the faintest hints of life, it converts the very pulses of the air into revelations." [2] It must not be burdened with too many facts, else the novelist instead of exercising his rightful function becomes a mere recorder. Even Balzac's imagination, great as it was, found itself hampered by his passion for facts, his obsession with the actual, which is the main flaw in his work. It is excess of material again that would interfere with a novelist's use of *The Ring and the Book*.

The idea but half hinted — when it is a very good one — is apt to contain the germ of happier fruit than the freight of the whole branch, waved at us or dropped into our lap, very often proves. This happens when we take over, as the phrase is, established data, take them over from existing records and under some involved obligation to take them as they stand. That drawback rests heavily for instance on the so-called historic fiction — so beautiful a case it is of a muddlement of terms — and is just one of the eminent reasons why the embarrassed Muse of that form, pulled up again and again, and the more often the fine intelligence invokes her, by the need of a superior harmony which shall be after all but a superior truth, catches up her flurried skirts and makes her saving dash for some gap in the hedge of romance. [3]

For it must be remembered that "life has no direct sense whatever for the subject," [4] that the observed reality becomes a subject only by being submitted to an imaginative

1. *The Princess Casamassima*, Preface, p. xxi.
2. "The Art of Fiction," *Partial Portraits*, p. 388.
3. *Notes on Novelists*, pp. 393, 394.
4. *The Spoils of Poynton*, Preface, p. vi.

process. Only when a hint, the smaller the better, offered by life has been "washed free of awkward accretions and hammered into a sacred hardness" does it become the "very stuff for a clear affirmation, the happiest chance for the indestructible." [1] The truest realism is "the real most finely mixed with life, which *is* in the last analysis the ideal," [2] and the work of the artist is the "aid given to true meanings to be born." [3] He can lead us, after all, only "into his own mind, his own vision of things"; [4] he must be a poet as well as an observer, poetry being "what helpful imagination, in however slight a dose, ever directly makes for." [5] Thus it is the great value of Daudet and Turgénieff that they were at once poets and realists, or realists in the best sense, and of the former James observes, "It is the real — the transmuted real — that he gives us best; the fruit of a process that adds to observation what a kiss adds to a greeting." [6] He disclaims any realistic intention, in the ordinary sense of the word, for his own "literary" stories, like "The Death of the Lion," admitting that they have been "drawn preponderantly from the depths of the designer's own mind," and "can be intelligently fathered but on his own intimate experience." [7] This whole point of view is, as we have seen, a guiding motive everywhere in James's criticism, in the early conclusions about Trollope, as in his view of the French Naturalists from first to last.

Imagination in any degree makes always for an idealization of reality, for poetry and romance, and the usual

1. *The Spoils of Poynton*, Preface, p. vi.
2. *Notes on Novelists*, p. 396.
3. *The Lesson of the Master*, Preface, p. ii.
4. *Picture and Text*, p. 151.
5. *Daisy Miller*, Preface, p. viii.
6. *Partial Portraits*, p. 217.
7. *The Lesson of the Master*, Preface, p. ix.

sharp distinction between realistic and romantic is a clumsy account of a subtle and complex relationship. In the great writer realism and romance are mixed; "he commits himself," says James, "in both directions, not quite at the same time nor to the same effect, of course, but by some need of performing his whole possible revolution, by the law of some rich passion in him for extremes. . . . His current remains therefore extraordinarily rich and mixed, washing us successively with the warm wave of the near and familiar and the tonic shock, as may be, of the far and strange." [1] In either case he can lead us only into his own vision of things, which is, at its best, "the state of private intercourse with things, the kind of current that in a given personal experinece flows to and fro between the imagination and the world." [2] For Rostand the romantic is the extravagant, but a far happier kind of romance is exhibited in D'Annunzio's *Virgins of the Rocks*.

. . . for if its tone is thoroughly romantic the romance is yet of the happiest kind, the kind that consists in the imaginative development of observable things, things present, significant, related to us, and not in a weak false fumble for the remote and the disconnected.[3]

Thus the true romantic is not necessarily the far and strange; it consists rather of the things that we can never directly experience except as a movement of our own minds, the things "that can reach us only through the beautiful circuit and subterfuge of our thought and our desire." [4] It

---

1. *The American*, Preface, p. xv. Compare what Scherer says of Flaubert's *L'Éducation Sentimentale*, "L'idéalisme et le réalisme ne sont donc pas deux manières d'entendre l'art, ce sont deux pôles entre lesquels tout art se meut . . . en dehors desquels il n'y a plus qu' abstraction stérile ou non moins stérile reproduction." *La Littérature Contemporaine*, iv, 294.
2. *Notes on Novelists*, p. 281.
3. *Ibid.*, p. 278. The same idea occurs in the early reviews.
4. *The American*, Preface, p. xvii.

is experience "disengaged,"_an inner state, yet after all but another face of the real. In the imaginative mind it is an activity which moves away from the observed reality towards an ideal construction, of which the elements are form and meaning in the widest possible sense, the order, lucidity, and suggestiveness for which life itself offers no parallel. Imagination may go far without abandoning its tie with the real, and when at last the severance is made the fact must not be apparent, for otherwise romance in failing to produce any illusion or to command any degree of intensity would fail to move us. "The balloon of experience," writes James, "is in fact of course tied to the earth, and under that necessity we swing, thanks to a rope of remarkable length, in the more or less commodious car of the imagination; but it is by the rope we know where we are, and from the moment that cable is cut we are at large and unrelated. The art of the romancer is 'for the fun of it' insidiously to cut the cable, to cut it without our detecting him." [1] As examples of the disconnected and liberated experience of romance James cites *Daisy Miller*,— Daisy herself being described as "pure poetry,"— *The American*, and *The Aspern Papers*. Concerning the last he observes that Jeffrey Aspern's only "link with reality" lies in the atmosphere, "in the tone of the picture wrought round him," which is itself an "artistic hokus-pokus," [2] as unreal as the character himself, but which on that very account helps the illusion and makes the whole semblance plausible. The point is that no question of reality is involved, but only a question as to the completeness of illusion. The surroundings therefore must be of a piece with the character, and the illusion succeeds, if at all, by being complete, by multiplying deceptions, by existing in its own right as a world apart.

1. *The American*, Preface, p. xviii.
2. *The Aspern Papers*, Preface, p. xiii.

92

James is far from denying that the novelist must have his facts, and he dwells much upon the value of "saturation," upon that inexhaustibly informed state which is the merit of Balzac and outweighs all his defects. The saturation is frequently most efficacious in a writer when it is local, greatly confined and verging on the provincial, as in Ibsen, in Dumas, in de Maupassant, and in Balzac himself. Thus he writes of Dumas, not perhaps without a strain of envy:

> The things close about him were the things he saw — there were alternatives, differences, opposites, of which he lacked so much as the suspicion. Nothing contributes more to the prompt fortune of an artist than some such positive and exclusive temper, the courage of his convictions, as we usually call it, the power to neglect something thoroughly, to abound aggressively in his own sense and express without reserve his own saturation. The saturation of the author of "Le Demi-Monde" was never far to seek. He was as native to Paris as a nectarine to a south wall.[1]

He was possibly encouraged, as Mr. Van Wyck Brooks suggests,[2] in his own effort to achieve a "local concentration" by Zola's success in "working up" his subjects, and he alludes in a notice of Henry Harland [3] more or less hopefully to the problem of the expatriated novelist, who may find in a shrinking world that the ancient local concentration of a Dickens or a Balzac is after all not indispensable to success. But he does not lose sight of the value of direct experience. "Art," he writes, "deals with what we see; it must first contribute full-handed that ingredient . . ." [4]

Something new and valuable in English fiction is this appetite for the real,[5] the "closeness of notation" of the

1. *Notes on Novelists*, pp. 369, 370.
2. *The Pilgrimage of Henry James*, p. 67.
3. "The Story-Teller at Large," *Fortnightly Review*, April, 1898.
4. *The Ambassadors*, Preface, p. ix.
5. *Notes on Novelists*, pp. 319 ff.

younger school of novelists, of Wells and Bennett and their disciples. They achieve value by saturation, and this is something in itself, even if their achievement of anything else is doubtful. Never before in the history of the English novel has there been so lively a consciousness of the importance of knowledge of every kind, of the fullest documentation, so determined and successful an effort to "hug the shore of the real," and this, so far as it goes, is to James's mind an advance. But the fatal flaw of the works produced in this spirit is that they are unselective, uncomposed, without intention or form. They have no controlling idea and seem to be unaware of the existence of method, which is the only thing that can make an intention entirely visible or turn the material of life to any artistic account. The most eminent example of an abundance of waste is Tolstoy,[1] whom the English novelists seem to have adopted as a model. They would have done better to study Turgénieff, who is both a realist and an artist. A good novel is not so much a slice of life as an extract, distilled by art, a thing shaped and wrought to some perceptible end, having a definable subject or idea and the degree of successful form needed to illustrate it. The "new novel" lacks both, and the course it has taken in Wells and Bennett leads absolutely nowhere. The slice of life theory conceived as a negation of purpose, method, and selection will not bear analysis.

There being no question of a slice upon which the further question of where and how to cut it does not wait, the office of method, the idea of choice and comparison, have occupied the ground from the first. This makes clear, to a moment's reflection, that there can be no such thing as an amorphous slice, and that any waving aside of inquiry as to the sense and value of a chunk of matter has to reckon with the simple truth of its having been

1. *Letters*, ii, 237.

born of naught else but measured excision. Reasons have been the fairies waiting on its cradle, the possible presence of a bad fairy in the form of a bad reason to the contrary notwithstanding. It has thus had connections at the very first stage of its detachment that are at no later stage logically to be repudiated; let it lie as lumpish as it will — for adoption, we mean, of the ideal of the lump — it has been tainted from too far back with the hard liability to form, and thus carries in its very breast the hapless contradiction of its sturdy claim to have none. This claim has the inevitable challenge at once to meet. How can a slice of life be anything but illustrational of the loaf, and how can illustration not immediately bristle with every sign of the extracted and related state? [1]

Disregard of form leads among other things to an abuse of dialogue, and this worst kind of looseness has taken the place of composition and structure. [2] Dialogue is valid only when it is illustrative, when it has been prepared for, related, supplied with a medium. In general it is to be used sparingly as in Conrad's *Chance* or in Mrs. Wharton's *Custom of the Country*, where we find dialogue "flowering, not weeding." It is apt to crowd out "the golden blocks themselves of the structure, the whole divine exercise and mystery of the exquisite art of presentation." [3] It is fatal unless it is merely illustrative of "something given us by another method, something constituted and presented." Worst of all is its baleful effect on the "sense of duration, the lapse and accumulation of time," which is the novelist's most difficult problem. But the unsparing use of dialogue is justified when it is itself the principle of structure in a novel, when it is arranged and "fundamentally organized to speak for itself," as in *The Awkward Age* and in Meredith's *Egoist*.

1. *Notes on Novelists*, p. 342.
2. *Ibid.*, pp. 351 ff.
3. *Ibid.*, p. 441. See also *The Awkward Age*, Preface, p. xvi.

The idea of a story is some more or less general truth about human life, a truth or meaning residing in the particular case with which the story deals. It can be expressed usually in a sentence or two. It has a strict and inherent logic, which determines the form of the story, which "holds up a candle to composition." The artist arrives at his truth and its special logic by analysis; observation having done its part in giving him the initial hint, his intelligence must do the rest.[1] By a process of imaginative incubation he must reveal to himself the full meaning of his case, its full illustrative value; he must "guess the unseen from the seen" and extract from the hopeless tangle of life a clear pattern of meaning. To the real artist this activity is the very breath of life, and in his capacity for disinterested wonder, in his passion for meaning he is a man apart. It opens up a realm of intellectual adventure which makes any other kind of adventure seem pale. "No privilege of the teller of tales," writes James, "has more the suspense and the thrill of a game of difficulty breathlessly played than just this business of looking for the unseen and the occult."[2] There is nothing in the prefaces about which James is more eloquent.

Sketchily clustered even, these elements gave out that vague pictorial glow which forms the first appeal of a living "subject" to the painter's consciousness; but the glimmer became intense as I proceeded to a further analysis. The further analysis is for that matter almost always the torch of rapture and victory, as the artist's firm hand grasps and plays it — I mean, naturally, of the smothered rapture and the obscure victory, enjoyed and celebrated not in the street but before some innermost shrine; the odds being a hundred to one, in almost any connexion, that it does n't arrive by any easy first process at the *best* residuum

1. Compare Charlotte Brontë's "We only suffer reality to *suggest*, never to *dictate*." Mrs. Gaskell's *Life*, p. 374.
2. *The Ambassadors*, Preface, p. ix.

of truth. That was the charm, sensibly, of the picture thus at first confusedly showing; the elements so could n't but flush, to their very surface, with some deeper depth of irony than the mere obvious. It lurked in the crude postulate like a buried scent; the more the attention hovered the more aware it became of the fragrance. To which I may add that the more I scratched the surface and penetrated, the more potent, to the intellectual nostril, became this virtue. At last, accordingly, the residuum, as I have called it, reached, I was in the presence of the red dramatic spark that glowed at the core of my vision and that, as I gently blew upon it, burned higher and clearer. This precious particle was the *full* ironic truth — the most interesting item to be read into the child's situation.[1]

A story should have, as the clue to its form, what James calls a "compositional centre," and the novelist's first care in reconstructing *The Ring and the Book*, for example, would be to provide himself with such a centre in the person of Caponsacchi.

To lift our subject out of the sphere of anecdote and place it in the sphere of drama, liberally considered, to give it dignity by extracting its finest importance, causing its parts to flower together into some splendid special sense, we supply it with a large lucid reflector, which we find only, as I have already noted, in that mind and soul concerned in the business that have at once the highest sensibility and the highest capacity, or that are, as we may call it, most admirably agitated.[2]

It is only through the "large lucid reflector," the "acute central consciousness" that the values of a story can be fully expressed and the unity of the subject manifested. If it be objected that the method is indirect, James urges that the indirectness is "that magnificent and masterly *indirectness* which means the *only* dramatic straightness and intensity."[3] When novelists like Balzac and Tolstoy

1. *What Maisie Knew*, Preface, p. vi.
2. *Notes on Novelists*, pp. 405, 406.   3. *Letters*, i, 322.

97

refuse to confine themselves in this way to a single point of view, it is because the complexity of their material forces them, for the sake of clearness, to try "again and again for new centres."[1] And they do not always succeed in being clear. The commonest form of the single point of view is, of course, the autobiographic, but to this James is strongly averse, for the reason that it "puts a premium on the loose, the improvised, the cheap and the easy";[2] it fails of "a rounded objectivity, of a precious effect of perspective, indispensable to beauty and authenticity."[3] It suffers from the "fluidity of self-revelation."

James's faith in the "central consciousness" arises from his belief that the interest of an action depends upon the character of the person acting. "I could think so little," he writes, "of any situation that didn't depend for its interest upon the nature of the persons situated and thereby on their way of taking it," and on the other hand "the agents in any drama are interesting only in proportion as they feel their respective situations; since the consciousness, on their part, of the complication exhibited forms for us their link of connection with it."[4] It is the fact that characters are "finely aware," as Hamlet and Lear are finely aware, that "*makes* absolutely the intensity of their adventure, gives the maximum of sense to what befalls them." For in art, the distinction between doing and feeling is unreal, and to talk of novels of character as opposed to novels of action seemed to James quite beside the mark. "What is character," he asks, "but the determination of incident? What is incident but the illustration of character? . . . It is an incident for a woman to stand up with her hand resting on a table and look out at you in a certain way. . . ."[5]

1. *Letters*, i, 327.   2. *Ibid.*, ii, 181.   3. *Ibid.*, p. 334.
4. *The Princess Casamassima*, Preface, p. vii.
5. "The Art of Fiction," *Partial Portraits*, p. 392.

In life we are more interested in results than in motives, in whatever produces a change in the balance of things confronting us and calls for adjustment. If we see a man creeping up behind us with a knife in his hand and a certain look in his eye, we do not stop to ascertain his motives or to admire the grace with which he moves. But observing the same man in the pages of a book we should have the liveliest interest in just these things, so negligible from a practical point of view. Art provides only for appreciation, for seeing and understanding; and doing and feeling tend to melt together in the spectator's sense or savoring of a situation. "What a man thinks," says James, "and what he feels are the history and character of what he does." [1]

It is, not surprisingly, one of the rudiments of criticism that a human, a personal "adventure" is no *a priori*, no positive and absolute and inelastic thing, but just a matter of relation and appreciation — a name we conveniently give, after the fact, to any passage, to any situation, that has added the sharp taste of uncertainty to a quickened sense of life. Therefore the thing is, all beautifully, a matter of interpretation and of the particular conditions; without a view of which latter some of the most prodigious adventures . . . may vulgarly show for nothing.[2]

A woman's standing up and looking out at you in a certain way is an incident for James because his attention is fixed upon the mental process behind the look, which, in his view, is all that makes it intelligible or interesting. If the same woman were to fling herself out of a third story window, the character of James's attention, as an artist, would remain exactly the same; it would still be fixed upon the motive, upon the complexion of mind which accompanied the act and determined its meaning. Interest in the act for itself, apart from motive or meaning, speaking always

1. *The Princess Casamassima*, Preface, p. xi.
2. *Daisy Miller*, Preface, p. xxiii.

in terms of art where nothing is to be done, belongs more to the gaping wonder of a child or a savage than to the intelligent curiosity of an artist. Nothing seems to James more admirable in D'Annunzio than his close notation of mental states, his preoccupation with psychology.[1]

Most people do not know what is happening to them and do not care. It is for those who do know, who can feel and understand that the artist reserves his sympathy and curiosity, caring "comparatively little for what happens to the stupid, the coarse, and the blind," except in so far as "the tangle, the drama, the tragedy and comedy of those who appreciate consists of their relation with those who don't." [2] The best of all subjects are those that "reside in somebody's excited and concentrated feeling about something — both the something and the somebody being of course as important as possible," such subjects having "more beauty to give out than under any other style of pressure." [3] To penetrate to the motives and perceptions of "those who appreciate" is like "cutting into the rich density of wedding cake." It is to come in contact with a fine throbbing undercurrent, which moves unrestingly, often deep below the surface, it offers mystery and suspense, it is a challenge to the artist's curiosity, and in producing a multiplication of meanings it provides for intensity and the sense of life.

A consciousness of this kind at the centre of the story, reflecting all its values, is to James the first law of structural economy, of method. But it is more than this, for the lucid reflector is no mere technical device but the very substance of James's art. It is a character who is "richly responsible" as well as "finely aware," the chief person in the story, and

1. *Notes on Novelists*, p. 257.
2. *The Princess Casamassima*, Preface, p. viii.
3. *The Spoils of Poynton*, Preface, pp. xiii, xiv.

by the same stroke a triumph of method and a triumph of value. Its fineness creates the predicament upon which the story hangs, and in dealing with this predicament the character's lucidity and passion play upon and intensify each other; awareness heightens responsibility, and both are supposed to lend a high dramatic value to conduct by making it difficult and precarious. Perhaps the best example in literature of this type of character is Hamlet. And the predicament in which the "free spirit" ordinarily finds itself is created by its relations with people who are stupid, vulgar, or morally obtuse. "I recognize," writes James, "that the novelist with a weakness for that ground of appeal is foredoomed to a well-nigh extravagant insistence on the free spirit." The fine conscience, in other words, may not succeed in being plausible, but in that case, James argues, "more or less of the treasure is stored safe from the moment so fine an interpretation and criticism as that of Fleda Vetch [in *The Spoils of Poynton*] ... is applied without waste to the surrounding tangle." For the essential thing is "to lodge somewhere at the heart of one's complexity an irrepressible appreciation." [1] A lack of verisimilitude in the principal character will not matter so long as the subject is exhibited.

It is easy to see why James found Emma Bovary insufficient, as a vessel of experience, to save the "dignity" of Flaubert's novel; why for the same reason he regarded *L'Éducation Sentimentale* as a complete failure. [2] The absence of the "complicated character" confronts him everywhere as the ugly and sometimes fatal defect in the work of Flaubert, de Maupassant, D'Annunzio, and others. It all comes back to richness of inspiration, to the artist's "psychological range." The writers mentioned could not

1. *The Spoils of Poynton*, Preface, p. xv.
2. *Notes on Novelists*, p. 82.

approach the complicated character because they had no
sense for the finer issues of life, and nothing about Flaubert is to James's mind more significant than his one attempt in this direction, in Mme. Arnoux of *L'Éducation*,
and its failure. If it be urged that Emma Bovary is perfectly adequate to the subject of the novel, James's
answer is that the subject itself and Flaubert's purpose
must then be considered inferior.

This is the point at which "moral sense and artistic
sense" lie very near together, in the range and quality of
the artist's feeling for life, the emphasis being upon quality. Without art the best intentions count for nothing, for
"the content and importance of a work of art are in fine
wholly dependent on its *being* one; outside of which all
prate of its representative character, its meaning and its
bearing, its morality and humanity is an impudent thing." [1]
The real artist has an identity "as marked as a window-
frame," and this identity, the range of vision, "proves
ever what it has *had* to be," [2] and to quarrel with it is useless. "It is the blessing of the art [of fiction] that it is made
up of experience conditioned infinitely in this personal
way. . . ." [3] And it is for this reason that the novel remains
still "the most independent, most elastic, most prodigious
of literary forms.[4] It permits of an infinitely greater "am-
plitude of protrayal" than the drama, and is in almost
every way the superior form. "It is the nature of the
theatre," writes James, "to give its victims, in exchange
for melancholy concessions, a vision of the immediate not
to be enjoyed in any other way; and consequently when the
material offered it to deal with is not the immediate but the

1. *The American*, Preface, p. xxi.
2. *Lady Barbarina*, Preface, p. viii.
3. "Kipling," *Views and Reviews*, p. 228.
4. *The Ambassadors*, Preface, p. xxiii.

contingent, the derived, the hypothetic, our melancholy concessions have been made in vain and the inadequacy of the form comes out." [1] The capacity of the novel, on the other hand, is unlimited.

We see this truth made strong, from beginning to end, in Zola's work: we see the temperament, we see the whole man, with his size and all his marks, stored and packed away in the huge hold of Les Rougon-Macquart as a cargo is packed away on a ship. His personality is the thing that finally pervades and prevails, just as so often on a vessel the presence of the cargo makes itself felt for the assaulted senses. What has most come home to me in reading him over is that a scheme of fiction so conducted is in fact a capacious vessel. It can carry anything — with art and force in the stowage; nothing in this case will sink it. And it is the only form for which such a claim can be made. All others have to confess to a smaller scope — to selection, to exclusion, to the danger of distortion, explosion, combustion. The novel has nothing to fear but sailing too light. It will take aboard all we bring in good faith to the dock. [2]

The novelist's freedom is boundless, and it is just this freedom that enables us to take his measure and express his " 'moral' reference."

The house of fiction has in short not one window but a million . . . every one of which has been pierced . . . by the need of the individual vision. . . . These apertures . . . hang so, all together, over the human scene . . . the human scene is the "choice of subject"; the . . . aperture . . . is the "literary form"; but they are as nothing without the posted presence of the watcher—without the consciousness of the artist. Tell me what the artist is, and I will tell you of what he has *been* conscious. Thereby I shall express to you at once his boundless freedom and his "moral" reference. [3]

The point as to dignity of subject may be illustrated by James's comment upon the criticism of one of his own stories. *What Maisie Knew* is a sordid tale of marital infi-

1. *Notes on Novelists*, p. 377. See *ante*, p. 37.
2. *Ibid.*, pp. 29, 30.   3. *The Portrait of a Lady*, Preface, p. x.

delity leading to the divorce court. Maisie, the child, is to live, by the court's verdict, for six months at a time, first with one parent, then with the other. Neither is capable of tenderness towards her, and each, promptly establishing another relationship, regards Maisie as a hateful encumbrance. She remains a link between the two establishments, however, and so brings about a new connection between the man and woman who appear on the scene after the divorce, and who have hitherto been unacquainted with each other. The point of the story lies in revealing this tangle of deceit and corruption through the innocent consciousness of a very sensitive and intelligent child. In itself the story of Maisie's parents is, James notes, "vulgar and empty." The chief characters are stupid and ignoble, "too poor for conversion" to the uses of art, the air surrounding them is "infected." But all this becomes "vivid, special, wrought hard"; it becomes "the stuff of poetry, tragedy and art"; it begins to have "meanings and connections with the universal," all by virtue of a single fact, Maisie's "freshness," her innocent, fluttering, acutely intelligent wonder. "For nobody," says James, "to whom life at large is easily interesting do the finer, shyer, the more anxious small vibrations, fine and shy and anxious with the passion that precedes knowledge, succeed in being negligible." [1] There lies the intensity, the importance, the solidity — in the numerous and delicate motions of the child's intelligence as it vibrates in that infected "air." These motions constitute to James's mind a large measure of "felt life"; they reach out in many directions, and the subect has a corresponding dignity and breadth of moral reference.

The foregoing, though it deals scarcely at all with the special technique expounded in the prefaces, is perhaps

1. *What Maisie Knew*, Preface, pp. xii, xiv.

sufficient to show what were James's ideas about the novel and art in general. The technique — which need not be analyzed here — can be summed up in a phrase as the law of entire expression, a severe principle of economy which has numerous and far-reaching implications, and is dominated by the strictest logic. Concerning the more general ideas there is, as we have seen, little in the prefaces that is not more or less clearly anticipated in James's earlier work, even as far back as the early reviews. His morality and idealism, his faith in the logic of art, and the discipline of form, an intellectual toughness, an emotional reserve, and a sensibility rather narrow but deep both as to life and literature, all this may be discerned in James from the first. Again, "The Art of Fiction" is perfectly consonant with the prefaces, though written some twenty years earlier; and so too is the whole of his criticism. The value of the prefaces is that they gather up and relate and express with a grace that makes them literature all of James's thought upon criticism, art, and life, as well as the technique of fiction. Faith in the logic of imagination, in the validity and sufficiency of an inner process which is at once intellectual and imaginative, is perhaps the most conspicuous thing about his theory of art. And his faith in art itself was absolute, in art as of course the product of imagination, of a sense for life, but as the product no less of intelligence and taste. No writer has ever had a clearer and more deeply reasoned assurance of the logic of his function, and if such a command of logic were sufficient for all the purposes of art, James would come near to being the greatest of all novelists. But if the prefaces do not make him a great novelist, they do in certain respects make him a great critic; and they have the highest interest and value, as the "story of a story" and as a body of artistic doctrine.

This doctrine is consistently applied in *Notes on Novelists*.[1] There is little in the substance of the volume that is fundamentally new, though its style and its refinement of tact and skill in the handling of a subject give it a place apart in James's criticism. Over half the book is devoted to writers whom James had previously treated, Stevenson, Balzac, Flaubert, and George Sand. Its point of view continues to be that of the English-speaking consciousness and also, with a certain authority, that of the fellow-craftsman, a point of view which enables the critic, as in the essay on Flaubert, to rest adverse criticism upon a distinction between the general and the "literary" reader. It may be observed that, for his own stories, James demands as of right in the prefaces the utmost closeness of perusal, admitting of no concessions to the general reader. He occupies in this volume much the same ground as before, impatient of the esthetic backwardness of the English and conscious of a moral and human inadequacy in his French and Italian subjects. The English are victims of the "stupid superstition that the amiability of a story-teller is the amiability of the people he represents," [2] failing to distinguish between subject and intention. They are grossly indifferent to ideas, to criticism and intelligent appreciation of art. The French novel, on the other hand, exhibits (in 1899) a dreary sameness of subject, sex of course, which has the fatal result of limiting the exposition of character.[3] Dumas the younger is a professed moralist and on the

1. Consisting of essays published between 1895 and 1914. Other essays written during these years and not republished are: "Du Maurier," *Harper's Magazine*, September, 1897; "The Present Literary Situation in France," *North American Review*, October, 1899; "Edmond Rostand," *The Critic*, November, 1901.
2. "Kipling," *Views and Reviews*, p. 233.
3. "The Present Literary Situation in France," *North American Review*, October, 1899.

whole, in James's opinion, a successful one, yet his moral taste is not infallible.[1] Flaubert had no sense for the finer side of human nature; Zola "*has* to improvise for his moral and social world," having no means of knowing any but the grosser parts of life. The "taste of fineness" lies not in his work, but in the history of his effort, and not even George Sand's eloquence and humanity can conceal the imperfectness of her moral sense.[2]

But observations like these are of very minor weight, and they lose practically all their invidiousness in the free play of the critic's curiosity. He is patient, detached, extraordinarily searching and supple. No greater gift of analysis, accompanied by the same degree of imagination and a corresponding flexibility, grace and vividness of style, was ever employed in fixing a writer's identity. Everywhere we find the "luminous center and related aspects" in a tightly woven tissue of analysis without crack or division, and with all the effect of a complex and finely determined perspective. The luminous centre is the heart of the subject's mystery, ironic or paradoxical, as a sufficiently fine and deep truth is likely to be, and fruitful of some general truth about art. Thus the moral question assumes ever more subtly an esthetic, a well-nigh technical significance. In Balzac, for example, the central thing for "the critic worth his salt," the attaching perplexity is the fact that "the artist of the Comédie Humaine is half smothered by the historian," that Balzac's inner vision so often fails at a given point and "his attention ruthlessly transfers itself from inside to outside, from the centre of his subject to its circumference." That is Balzac's catastrophe, and the failure is proportionate to the greatness of his genius. Concerning the failure James draws a moral and makes a distinction, both highly characteristic.

1. *Notes on Novelists*, p. 375.   2. *Ibid.*, pp. 81 ff.; 38, 49; 204.

The genius this figure stands for, none the less, is really such a lesson to the artist as perfection itself would be powerless to give; it carries him so much further into the special mystery. Where it carries him, at the same time, I must not in this scant space attempt to say — which would be a loss of the fine thread of my argument. I stick to our point in putting it, more concisely, that the artist of the Comédie Humaine is half smothered by the historian. Yet it belongs as well to the matter also to meet the question of whether the historian himself may not be an artist — in which case Balzac's catastrophe would seem to lose its excuse. The answer of course is that the reporter, however philosophical, has one law, and the originator, however substantially fed, has another; so that the two laws can with no sort of harmony or congruity make, for the finer sense, a common household.

. . . .

The principle of composition that his free imagination would have, or certainly might have, handsomely imposed on him is perpetually dislocated by the quite opposite principle of the earnest seeker, the inquirer to a useful end, in whom nothing is free but a born antipathy to his yoke-fellow.[1]

Yet Balzac remains, in spite of his failure, the "first and foremost member of his craft, a Gulliver among pigmies." The elements, the raw materials of the criticism are much the same as in *French Poets and Novelists*, but while in the earlier book these elements are merely named and discussed, each more or less by itself, here they are related, or fused, qualified, and composed to the last degree. In this respect the difference is almost as great as between the early reviews and the best of the essays in *Partial Portraits*. Nothing could be more instructive as to critical style than a comparison of these earlier and later treatments of Balzac. This is how James describes Balzac's "cockneyism" in *French Poets* and in the *Notes:*

If Balzac had represented any other country than France, if his imagination had ever left a footprint in England or Germany, it is a matter of course for those who know him that his fathomless

1. *Notes on Novelists*, pp. 115, 116.

Parisian cockneyism would have had on these occasions a still sharper emphasis. But there is nothing to prove that he in the least "realized," as we say, the existence of England and Germany. That he had of course a complete theory of the British constitution and the German intellect makes little difference; for Balzac's theories were often in direct proportion to his ignorance. He never perceived with any especial directness that the civilized world was made up of something else than Paris and the provinces; and as he is said to have been able to persuade himself, by repeating it a few times, that he had done various things which he had not done — made a present of a white horse, for instance, to his publisher — so he would have had only to say often enough to himself that England was a mythic country to believe imperturbably that there was in fact, three hundred miles away, no magnificent far-spreading London to invalidate his constant assumption that Paris is the pivot of human history.[1]

He had indeed a striking good fortune, the only one he was to enjoy as an harassed and exasperated worker: the great garden of life presented itself to him absolutely and exactly in the guise of the great garden of France, a subject vast and comprehensive enough, yet with definite edges and corners. This identity of his universal with his local and national vision is the particular thing we should doubtless call his greatest strength were we preparing agreeably to speak of it also as his visible weakness. Of Balzac's weaknesses, however, it takes some assurance to talk; there is always plenty of time for them; they are the last signs we know him by — such things truly as in other painters of manners often come under the head of mere exuberance of energy. So little, in short, do they earn the invidious name even when we feel them as defects.

What he did above all was to read the universe, as hard and as loud as he could, *into* the France of his time; his own eyes regarding his work as at once the drama of man and a mirror of the mass of social phenomena the most rounded and registered, most organized and administered, and thereby most exposed to systematic observation and portrayal, that the world had seen.[2]

James's theory of a "case" is perhaps best illustrated in the essays on Zola and D'Annunzio. We are reminded of

1. *French Poets and Novelists*, p. 92.   2. *Notes on Novelists*, p. 112.

his early regret that for Zola the real meant always the unclean. In the present essay he insists upon Zola's sincerity, passion for truth and seriousness of intention. Those who can see nothing but the improper in him have far less sense of proportion than Zola himself. The important thing is that Zola did justice to his subject; his rejection of it would have been the "waste of a faculty." And it was precisely his great defect, his want of taste, that proved to be his greatest strength, for without his "stoutness of stomach" and his rank materialism, he could not have approached the subject at all. Is taste then not indispensable? In this particular case, up to a certain point, it was not; the lack of it was positively helpful; yet in the end — and this is what makes Zola an instructive case — the absence of taste led to a breakdown of the imagination itself, and the quality is supremely vindicated in Zola's ultimate failure.

This lesson may not, barely stated, sound remarkable; yet without being in possession of it I should have ventured on none of these remarks. "The matter with" Zola then, so far as it goes, was that, as the imagination of the artist is in the best cases not only clarified but intensified by his equal possession of Taste (deserving here if ever the old-fashioned honour of a capital) so when he has lucklessly never inherited that auxiliary blessing the imagination itself inevitably breaks down as a consequence. There is simply no limit, in fine, to the misfortune of being tasteless; it does not merely disfigure the surface and the fringe of your performance — it eats back into the very heart and enfeebles the sources of life. When you have no taste you have no discretion, which is the conscience of taste, and when you have no discretion you perpetrate books like "Rome," which are without intellectual modesty, books like "Fécondité," which are without a sense of the ridiculous, books like "Vérité," which are without the finer vision of human experience.[1]

1. *Notes on Novelists*, p. 49.

In its plan and conclusion the essay recalls the one on de Maupassant. But there is a striking difference. James is no longer the avowed moralist, the fusion between morality and esthetics is complete, in practice as well as in theory, and Zola's coarseness of vision, not after all very different from de Maupassant's, is consistently referred to an esthetic criterion, never for a moment to a moral one. For the rest James's sympathy with his subject is more pronounced, and the air of detachment in the essay is far more convincing. There is no trace of the patronizing compassion which he bestows on Flaubert's moral infirmities in *Essays in London*. He liked Zola as a man, liked his courage, honesty, industry, above all his devotion to his craft. He liked in Zola's work the qualities that reminded him of Balzac. The essay is a capital instance of James's analysis of a temperament from the point of view simply of its capacity to produce fiction. The analysis is progressive and dramatic; it presents the drama of a case, a drama, by James's account, more intense than that of any of Zola's stories. How did a given body of work come to be what it is? What is the nature of the mind that produced it? what are its inherent qualities, its history and surrounding air? The book is the man, and the office of the critic is to demonstrate the logic of literary character, to see every part in relation to the whole, to unfold and dissect, binding his demonstration together more neatly and firmly at every step. He holds the final clue in his hand, and is intent upon exposing every part of his subject as a function of the whole.

In *Notes on Novelists* James is more friendly towards Flaubert and far more just to him than in *Essays in London*. The earlier estimate is concerned chiefly with Flaubert's faults as a man, the later is occupied with his great qualities as a writer. It begins where the other leaves off. It does not ignore Flaubert's moral limitations, but it greatly minimizes their importance. "The limit of his range, and above all of his reach," writes the critic, "is ... sufficiently indicated, and yet perhaps in the event without injury to his name." [1] Nobody, we were told in the *Essays*, takes Flaubert's great question seriously, but in the present volume James points out that Flaubert "has fed and fertilized, has filtered through others," so that "the world at large possesses him not less than the *confrère*." He is a perfect case — typical, objective, simplified and fixed, "exhibitional and describable." One thing that makes him so is his passion for style and the proof he gives of what style can do, how it can triumph over the question of value. *Madame Bovary* shows "that a work of art may be markedly open to objection and at the same time be rare in its kind, and that when it is perfect to this point nothing else particularly matters." [2] It "confers on its sufficiently vulgar elements of exhibition a final unsurpassable form," and this is a thing almost unknown in English fiction.

They all represent the pursuit of a style, of the ideally right one for its relations, and would still be interesting if the style had not been achieved. "Madame Bovary," "Salammbô," "Saint Antoine," "L'Éducation," are so written and so composed (though the last-named in a minor degree) that the more we look at them the more we find in them, under this head, a beauty of intention and of effect; the more they figure in the too often dreary desert of fictional prose a class by themselves and a little living oasis. So far as that desert is of the complexion of our own English speech it supplies with remarkable rarity this particular source of refreshment. So strikingly is that the case, so scant for the most part any dreams of a scheme of beauty in these connections, that a critic betrayed at artless moments into a plea for composition may find himself as blankly met as if his plea were for trigonometry.[3]

1. *Notes on Novelists*, p. 68.   2. *Ibid.*, p. 80.
3. *Ibid.*, pp. 90, 91.

The whole essay is impartial, discerning, and eloquent, vindicating by the fineness of its insight the critic's right to speak as a "fellow-craftsman," firm in its English point of view, yet closely and sympathetically attentive to the special values of the subject.

The moral of a case, its artistic lesson, is nowhere more clearly revealed than in the essay on D'Annunzio, where also the critic's "special window" is as sharply defined as his subject's. James re-affirms here the critical position defined in "The Art of Fiction," and the essay is a complete illustration of it.

But we of course never play the fair critical game with an author, never get into relation with him at all, unless we grant him his postulates. His subject is what is given him — given him by influences, by a process, with which we have nothing to do; since what art, what revelation, can ever really make such a mystery, such a passage in the private life of the intellect, adequately traceable for us? His treatment of it, on the other hand, is what he actively gives; and it is with what he gives that we are critically concerned. If there is nothing in him that effectually induces us to make the postulate, he is then empty for us altogether, and the sooner we have done with him the better; little as the truly curious critic enjoys, as a general thing, having publicly to throw up the sponge.[1]

D'Annunzio is a perfect case, because he is a well defined temperament which succeeds in being completely expressive, and James rejoices in the critic's opportunity. "The great feast-days of all, for the restless critic, are those much interspaced occasions of his really meeting a 'case' . . ."[2] He recognizes it intuitively.

He may perhaps not always be able to give us the grounds of his certainty, but he is at least never without knowing it in presence of one of the full-blown products that are the joy of the

1. *Notes on Novelists*, p. 259.   2. *Ibid.*, p. 245.

analyst. He recognizes as well how the state of being full-blown comes above all from the achievement of consistency, of that last consistency which springs from the unrestricted enjoyment of freedom.[1]

What the case of D'Annunzio illustrates for James is the failure of estheticism, however complete or effective, when unaccompanied by a sense for human values, the failure of lovely appearances, of a consistent sacrifice to beauty, of style itself in the absence of the complicated character and the finer vision. D'Annunzio is a rare example because he is so fully equipped and unhampered in every direction but one. He shows for one thing to what extent the cult of the 'nineties in England, as an experiment in the esthetic, was a fumbling and timid failure, "surrounded and manipulated by as many different kinds of inexpertness as probably ever huddled together on a single pretext." [2] And he offers also, incidentally, a lesson in the true nature of the romantic.

His great qualities for James are his rare notation of states of excited sensibility, his visual sense, and his ample and exquisite style. There is a complete fusion in his work of substance and form. Yet all this cannot quite conceal the essential vulgarity of his spirit. His subject is always "the more or less insanely demoralized pair of lovers, for neither of whom is any other personal relation indicated either as actual or as conceivably possible," and his material is therefore "alarmingly cut down as to range, as to interest, and not least, as to charm." [3] The result seems somehow not to suffer, thanks to D'Annunzio's "magic," to his distinction of form. But the fact that he is all picture and no idea becomes more and more apparent and disturbing. We are aware of an "incessant *leak* in the effect of

1. *Notes on Novelists*, p. 246.   2. *Ibid.*
3. *Ibid.*, pp. 260, 261.

distinction so copiously and artfully produced." We see that the failure of the English experiment was due to the lack of a certain force of temperament which enables writers like D'Annunzio and Matilde Serao to work serenely in the faith that the sexual relation is of all others the most productive of beauty. But what, asks James, is this "queer passion" which has neither "duration, nor propagation, nor common kindness, nor congruity with the rest of life," nothing in short "to make its importance good"? Love in D'Annunzio is isolated and disconnected, it is only the act of a moment, it fails to exhibit character and to provide for inwardness. The distinction of the sexual passion, precarious at the best, is thus endangered, for the passion is interesting only for what it represents, for what a character makes of it; and D'Annunzio's characters have nothing to contribute. His whole citadel of beauty is undermined by an element of vulgarity. "The vulgarity comes from the disorder really introduced into values . . . from the vitiation suffered . . . by taste, impeccable taste itself."

This then is the moral of the esthetic adventure, that distinction of appearances is worth little without the more important inner distinction which depends upon beauty and richness of character. The same thing is even more conclusively demonstrated in Matilde Serao. That the English failed in the esthetic experiment is by no means to their discredit, and their conventional reticence about love is far better than a ruthless preoccupation with it and the suppression of everything else, a process which falsifies passion itself, as well as the "total show." Passion is interesting in proportion as it is "mixed with other things."

I think the exhibition of "Love" as "Love" — functional Love — always suffers from a certain inevitable and insurmountable flat-footedness (for the reader's nerves, etc.;) which is only to be counterplotted by roundabout arts — as by tracing it through indirectness and tortuosities of application and effect — to keep it somehow interesting and productive (though I don't mean *re*productive!). But this again is a big subject.[1]

Better our "fund of reserve," a "cool virtue," the "grace of hanging back," even a shade of the superficial. As between two misrepresentations of the world our own is better. Only a very fine sense can combine candor with delicacy; freedom is good only for the "very eminent." The English convention takes the place of the fine sense, which happens to be rare among writers of the day.[2] The esthetic adventure will be completely successful only, if ever, when the art of a writer like D'Annunzio is joined to a comparable degree of taste and spiritual sensibility. Meanwhile the English instinct of reticence is a precious thing, and "there would be no greater mistake than to attempt too simple an account of it."[3] It means much for "*our* culture" that an English hand would have been incapable of touching such material as the life of George Sand.[4] This is the English-speaking consciousness in James, exactly the same as in *Partial Portraits* and *Essays in London.*

His attitude towards provincialism is significant. He had always the sense, derived from Matthew Arnold and from the conditions of his own early life, of a traditional European culture, with its chief strongholds in Italy, France, and England, a code of manners, a system of values, and an ideal of civilized life which seemed to him essential for the production of literature. His allusions to provincialism are frequent. There was the esthetic provincialism of America, the social barbarity of the Scandinavian countries, the moral superficiality of the French, the absence

1. *Letters,* ii, 182.   2. *Notes on Novelists,* pp. 308 ff.
3. *Ibid.,* p. 297.   4. *Ibid.,* p. 190.

of cultural discipline among the Russians. Especially interesting because of its allusion to James himself as a "worshipper at the esthetic shrine *quand même*" is this comment on the imperfect esthetic emancipation of Charles Eliot Norton:

Nothing in fact *can* be more interesting to a hunter of other intellectual climes and a worshipper at the esthetic shrine *quand même* than to note once more how race and implanted quality and association always in the end come by their own; how for example a son of the Puritans the most intellectually transmuted, the most liberally emancipated and initiated possible, could still plead most for substance when proposing to plead for style, could still try to lose himself in the labyrinth of delight while keeping tight hold of the clue of duty, tangled even a little in his feet; could still address himself all consistently to the moral conscience while speaking as by his office for our imagination and our free curiosity.[1]

Is the restriction altogether inapplicable to the critic himself? He is struck by the contrast between Ibsen's mastery of form and "the bareness and bleakness of his little northern democracy," where apparently there is no "small-talk" and "scarcely any manners." Ibsen's success in these surroundings, with "so indifferent a vision of the comedy of things," and by help of the provincial waste itself is a curiosity and a miracle.[2] Again the provincialism of the Russians is illustrated in Mme. Karénine's unselective and diffuse biography of George Sand, with its "psychological intelligence and lame esthetic," [3] as also of course in the "loose baggy monsters" produced under the name of novels by Tolstoy and Dostoieffsky.

An ideal of manners, of right feeling and conduct was involved for James in the question of the artist's privacy. He tells us that in general "artists are well advised to

1. *Notes on Novelists*, p. 422.　　2. *Ibid.*, pp. 425, 426.
3. *Ibid.*, pp. 189, 190.

cover their tracks." [1] He is always reluctant and apologetic about drawing aside the veil, upon such things, for example, as Flaubert's epileptic fits or George Sand's amours and domestic squabbles, though his reluctance does not prevent him from "picking a value" out of the mire when he can. What are the rights of the matter? The question is argued at some length in one of the essays on George Sand. [2] The plea of the "analyst" is that "when we wish to know at all we wish to know everything," and that not only the competence but the very decency of the observer depends upon his not being superficial. Yet "there is clean linen and soiled," and "life would be intolerable without some acknowledgment even by the pushing of such a thing as forbidden ground." Zola insists upon telling us everything about himself, strong in his conviction that the truth is never either ridiculous or unclean, but this conviction is "the result of a rare confusion between give and take, between 'truth' and information." James's distinction is subtle and thoroughly characteristic. The truth in such a case is no absolute thing but is determined by what has meaning and value for the receiving mind; its own necessity, its "simple necessity of feeling" may be on occasion "the truest thing of all." If the mind "feels more about a Zola functionally undeciphered it will be governed more by that particular truth than by the truth about his digestive idiosyncrasies." [3] It is only by selection that we can arrive at the best truth, at the truth which will have a maximum of value. "Nothing often is less superficial," writes James, "than to ignore and overlook, or more constructive (for living and feeling at all) than to want impatiently to choose." The necessity of feeling to which he alludes here, the dictates of imagination and taste, gov-

1. *Notes on Novelists*, p. 4.   2. *Ibid.*, pp. 165–169.
3. *Ibid.*, p. 167.

erned his whole attitude towards truth, both in his theory and practice of fiction, and in his autobiographical books.[1]

"The manner of the thing," writes James of "The Pupil," may thus illustrate the author's incorrigible taste for gradations and superpositions of effect," and explains why "he incurs the stigma of labouring uncannily for a certain fullness of truth."[2] In *Notes on Novelists* the manner of the thing gives the best of the essays something like the organic cohesion of a soap-bubble. The thought is carried over without a break from one division to the next, and the pauses are not so much divisions of thought as breathing spaces. It is more like the progress of rhythm in rise and fall than like the sharp articulation of structure. There are *eddies* rather than pauses in the movement of thought, points where a mingling of old and new occurs, something is repeated, something added, and then the new direction reveals itself. There are "fusions and interrelations," with "every part of the stuff encircled in every other." Every degree of the conditional and parenthetical, every manner of qualification is employed to produce a perspective which reminds one of Renan's famous comparison of the truth to the colors on a dove's neck. James could be infinitely true to his inner vision, and the prefaces and *Notes on Novelists* are likely to endure not only as fine examples of critical method but as a minor triumph of English prose.

It is perhaps unnecessary to repeat that the native bias of James's mind seems scarcely to have been touched by a very great deepening of esthetic insight and by the development of a supreme gift of expression. What change there was took the form of a complete logical fusion in him

1. See his justification of a departure from strict truth in his treatment of William James in *Notes of a Son and Brother, Letters*, ii, 346, 347.
2. Preface, p. xviii.

of a faith in art and a faith in conduct; his artistic conscience took charge of everything, and from a supervision so alert and sensitive morality could have had little to lose, and art much to gain perhaps. He could not have served two masters so well without a suppleness, almost an elusiveness, that makes him sometimes the despair of an attentive reader. He slips through the net, and one feels that scarcely any net but his own would be fine enough to hold him. The unity of his mind is the great fact, but it is a unity difficult to seize. He is, for example, in a sense the most intellectual of critics, and yet the least interested of all in general ideas. He puts art above life, yet no critic has urged the claims of conduct more eloquently or insisted more upon the bareness of an art for art doctrine. No one surely has ever had so strong a passion for literature together with so limited an appetite for books. His bias in criticism, like his style, is his own; he cannot be fitted into any category. He rejects standards, rules, classes, and types; he has his own standards, best of all his own taste, and he is not an impressionist, like Pater, for example. It is not the adventures of his soul that he records, but the visible, objective qualities of the thing before him; he is the analyst always, never merely the sensitive soul. If to be philosophical is to relate literature at many points to the greater interests of mankind, James is not a philosophical critic, yet no critic has ever gone more deeply into the philosophy of art. His opinions are often derivative; he was not likely to recognize genius in a strange guise or to make discoveries, for his taste was not adaptive. He was infinitely susceptible of inner adjustments but not of outer ones. Yet if his taste was narrow, a high degree of self-consciousness and an extraordinary analytical power enabled him always to discover the grounds of it; and for the rest, where his taste operated at all, it was sure and beautifully revealing.

BIBLIOGRAPHY

BIBLIOGRAPHY

I. Works of Henry James Referred to in this Study

Novels and Tales, New York, 1907–1917.
The Middle Years, New York, 1917.
Notes of a Son and Brother, New York, 1914.
A Small Boy and Others, New York, 1914.
Letters (2 vols.), New York, 1920.
Notes and Reviews, Cambridge, Massachusetts, 1921.
Views and Reviews (ed. by Le Roy Phillips), Boston, 1908.
French Poets and Novelists, London, 1878.
"Hawthorne," in English Men of Letters, London, 1879.
Partial Portraits, London, 1888.
Essays in London, New York, 1893.
Picture and Text, New York, 1893.
Notes on Novelists, New York, 1916.
A Bibliography of the Writings of Henry James. Le Roy Phillips, Boston and New York, 1906.

Note: Uncollected reviews and articles referred to in the text will be found listed in Mr. Phillips's bibliography.

II. Books and Articles on Henry James

Beach, Joseph Warren, The Method of Henry James. Yale University Press, 1918.
Bennett, Arnold, Books and Persons. London, 1917.
Benson, A. C., Memories and Friends. London, 1924.
Blanche, Jaques-Émile, "Henry James," in La Revue Européenne, August and September, 1923.
Bosanquet, Theodora, Henry James at Work. The Hogarth Press, London, 1924.
Bradford, Gamaliel, "Portrait of Henry James," in the North American Review, February, 1921.
Brooks, Van Wyck, The Pilgrimage of Henry James. New York, 1925.
Brownell, W. C., American Prose Masters. New York, 1909.

BIBLIOGRAPHY

Burton, Richard, Literary Likings. Boston, 1898.
Cary, Elizabeth L., Novels of Henry James. New York, 1905.
Appendix contains bibliography by F. A. King.
Conrad, Joseph "Henry James, An Appreciation," in the *North American Review*, April, 1916.
Edgar, Pelham, Henry James, Man and Author. Boston and New York, 1927.
Elton, Oliver, Modern Studies. London, 1907.
Follet, Wilson, The Modern Novel. New York, 1923.
Follet, Wilson, "The Simplicity of Henry James," in the *American Review*, May and June, 1923.
Fullerton, Morton, "The Art of Henry James," in the *Quarterly Review*, April, 1910.
Garnier, Marie-Reine, Henry James et la France. Paris, 1927.
Gosse, Edmund, "Henry James," in *Scribner's Magazine*, April, and May, 1920.
Gretton, M. S., "Henry James and his Prefaces," in the *Contemporary Review*, 101: 69–78.
Hale, E. E., "The Rejuvenation of Henry James," in *The Dial*, March 16, 1908.
Heuffer (Ford), Ford Madox, Henry James. London, 1913.
Howells, W. D., "Henry James's Later Work," in the *North American Review*, January, 1903.
Hughes, Herbert Leland, Theory and Practice in Henry James, University of Virginia, Dissertation.
Littell, P., "Henry James as a Critic," in the *New Republic*, November 21, 1914.
Lubbock, Percy, "Henry James," in the *Quarterly Review*. London, July, 1916.
Lubbock, Percy, The Craft of Fiction. London, 1921.
Macdonell, A., "Henry James as a Critic," in the *Bookman*, April, 1916.
McIntyre, Clara, "Henry James's Later Manner," in *Publications of the Modern Language Association*, vol. xx.
Palache, John G., "The Critical Faculty of Henry James," in the *University of California Chronicle*, xxvi (October, 1924), 4.
Perry, Bliss, "Commemorative Tribute to Henry James," in American Academy of Arts and Letters, 1921–22.
Phelps, W. L., James, Bryant, etc. New York, 1924.
Pound, Ezra, Instigations. New York, 1920.

BIBLIOGRAPHY

Preston, H. W., "The Latest Novels of Howells and James," in the *Atlantic Monthly*, January, 1903.

Randell, Wilfred, "The Art of Henry James," in the *Living Age*, July 29, 1916.

Scott, Dixon, Men of Letters. New York, 1923.

Sherman, Stuart P., On Contemporary Literature. New York, 1917.

Vedder, H. C., American Writers. Boston, 1895.

Waterlow, S. P., "The Work of Henry James," in the *Independent Review*, October, 1904; January, 1905.

West, Rebecca, Henry James. New York, 1916.

Wyatt, Edith, "Henry James, An Impression," in the *North American Review*, April, 1916.

INDEX

INDEX

129

INDEX

Howells, 83
Hugo, 9

Ibsen, 93, 117

James, Henry
Aim in criticism, 66, 67; in fiction, 64, 66, 67, 69
Apprenticeship in criticism, 4; period of real, 31
Art and life, 86 ff., 99 ff.
Autobiographical books, 16, 119
Career, beginning of, 3–28; transitional, 29–53; rounding out, 57–79; fulfilment, 83–120
Character, sense for, 79
Criticism, and fiction one art, 3; apprenticeship in, 4; beginning and end of writing career, 4; bent of early critical genius, 6; limited range, 7, 24; theory of, 11, 13 ff., 35, 57, 58, 60, 66 ff.; ultimate doctrine of, 24; advance in critical skill, 32; art of, 67; method of, 76, 77, 79, 86, 111, 113, 119; bias in, 120
Disciple of Sainte-Beuve, 79
Dominating preference, 8, 23, 51
Drama, interest in, 25, 26, 102
Early antipathies, 8; influences, 5, 7, 9, 10, 24
English bias, 22, 37, 40, 69, 75, 77, 116; London becomes permanent home, 31
Esthetic idealism, 23, 61, 110 ff., 115; insight, 119
European cities, atmosphere of, 84
Fiction, theory of, 16, 17, 19, 20, 26, 59, 60, 96 ff., 102 ff.; romance and novel, 20; realism, 21, 22, 23, 50, 90 ff.; style, 88; imagination and fact, 88 ff., 96; dialogue, 95; idea of a story, 96; compositional cen-

tre, 97; point of view, 97; reflecting consciousness, 100 ff.; technique, 105
First appearance in print, 4
Form, interest in, 20, 24, 25, 60, 87 ff., 94 ff., 97, 112, 114; and content, 60, 87, 88
French Naturalism, 22, 39, 41 ff., 61, 62, 69, 71, 78, 90
French people, attitude towards, 36 ff., 62, 68, 106; literature, attitude towards, 36, 38 ff., 68, 69; liberalizing effect of, 26
Importance of subject, 24, 36, 44, 58, 100
Important and productive decade (1873–1883), 31
Interest in dramatic technique, 25, 26, 102; technical difficulties a challenge, 25
Moral temper, 14, 23, 24, 36 ff., 44 ff., 60 ff. ,67, 69, 102 ff., 107, 110, 112, 114
New England heritage, 4, 9, 37, 53
Paris, residence in, 38, 40; literary group of, 38 ff.
Parisian stage, 39
Philosophy of life, 5
Poetry, taste in, 24, 50, 51
Provincialism, attitude towards, 41, 52, 78, 116, 117
Reading, 6, 50, 120
Realistic bent in literature, 22
Saturation, value of, 93
Style, 3, 52
Truth, fineness of, 67; novel's foremost claim to merit, 19, 24; and information, distinction between, 118, 119
James, Henry, Sr., 13

Karénine, Madame, 117
Kingsley, Charles, 27

INDEX